AN INTRODUCTION TO ORACY

Frameworks for Talk

Edited by

Jackie Holderness and Barbara Lalljee

CASSELL

Cassell
Wellington House
125 Strand, London WC2R 0BB

PO Box 605
Herndon, VA 20172

First published 1998

British Library Cataloguing-in-Publication Data
A catalogue record for this book is available from the British Library.

ISBN 0-304-33950-4 (paperback)
     0-304-33949-0 (hardback)

Typeset by Kenneth Burnley in Irby, Wirral, Cheshire.
Printed and bound in Great Britain by Redwood Books, Trowbridge, Wiltshire.

Contents

Introduction

Talking About Talk

When children and adults talk, they translate their ideas and feelings into sounds. Talk is affected, shaped and determined by numerous factors, many of them not immediately obvious. They include the senses, the environment, relationships, our conceptual understanding and our body language. Talk can appear difficult to plan for, complex to manage and impossible to measure accurately.

Traditionally, in school, children have listened more than they have talked. The National Curriculum has done much to point up the importance of oracy and has emphasized the need to extend the range of purposes open to children for different kinds of talk. The National Curriculum requires teachers to develop key skills of communication and effective listening. Children must also be introduced to the importance of Standard English.

While many of these requirements will be satisfied incidentally across a rich and broad curriculum, most teachers find it is essential to structure their planning for oracy in order to guarantee coherence, progression, continuity and the systematic development of crucial skills. Such planning must also build in provision for regular monitoring of children's achievements in oracy within a wide range of contexts.

This book contains a variety of perspectives on providing frameworks to support children's speaking and listening. The approaches and topics included have all grown out of classroom practice and represent successful attempts by teachers to structure oracy activities. With an emphasis on increasing children's participation, the contributors look at issues surrounding oracy in schools and offer useful frameworks for talk.

PLANNING

Many teachers plan for different types of English work but this does not always include detailed plans for speaking and listening. Planning for talk is as important as planning for any other English activity.

This book provides rationales, strategies and frameworks for planning for talk. These can be integrated into whatever model of planning has been adopted or used to complement a daily Literacy Hour.

GROUPING

Self-esteem is central to a child's ability to convey meaning confidently. Many teachers use Circle Time effectively to encourage children to discuss issues of interest, and learn to debate and challenge one another in a supportive setting. Circle Time is the name given to a regular whole-class discussion where the whole class sits in a circle so that each pupil can see everyone's face (including the teacher). Teachers and children use it as a forum for discussion, having agreed ground rules for participation.

Class assemblies frequently allow teachers and children to discuss topics of personal interest, celebrate what makes each individual unique and valuable, and explore ideas and shared values.

In classes of ever-increasing size, there is more pressure to return to whole-class teaching. Whole-class teaching is of course entirely appropriate for some teaching and learning, but it does not always enable children to articulate their ideas effectively, and can reduce the length and quality of pupil contribution in discussion. Teachers who are sensitive to children's attempts to express themselves, realize the importance of small group and pair work in which all children can share and justify their opinions, ask questions and explore ideas (see Chapters 1 and 4).

EQUAL OPPORTUNITIES

It is hard to ensure equal access to the oracy curriculum, if only because some children are more inclined to 'hold the floor' than others. Most teachers are aware of the occasional need to engineer mixed groups (mixed according to ability, gender or even ethnic group) so that children are challenged by others' points of view and encouraged to listen responsively to others' contributions. When working as part of a group which includes native English speakers, EAL children are provided with models of language in context and are actively assimilated into the social world of the classroom.

Chapters 1, 3, 4, 9 and 11 are particularly designed to increase individual participation.

INFORMATION AND COMMUNICATION TECHNOLOGY

Although there is no specific chapter on the importance of the computer in oracy work, it is assumed and hoped that teachers already appreciate the value of having more than one child working at a computer task on the screen or with the roamer. The shared challenges and experiences offer genuine reasons to negotiate solutions, predict outcomes and confirm and describe results.

BOOKTALK

Reading and discussing books are daily events in most primary classrooms and provide opportunities for pair work and group work which can encompass a wide range of talk. Once established, group reading sessions, in which a small group read and debate multiple copies of the same text, can enable the adult to step back and listen, observing and recording the children as they compare the text with others, debate motives, make predictions, express feelings and justify opinions. The chapters which build upon this practice are Chapters 6 and 8.

STAFF DEVELOPMENT

Most schools may have already looked at oracy in some depth, as part of a rolling in-service programme about English. The work of the National Oracy Project (1988–1991) has been invaluable in guiding and supporting teachers' understanding of the nature of talk. LINC (Language in the National Curriculum) groups around the country provided workshops to enhance oracy work in schools. Nearly all INSET sessions about oracy encourage teachers to become more reflective about their own teacher talk and to become critically aware of their interactions with their pupils.

Colleagues may find the following questions helpful in reflecting upon their current oracy practice.

- Which speaking and listening behaviours are already established and followed? Is there a school-wide policy?

- How do children listen and respond to teachers and to other adults?

- How do they listen and respond to each other?

- How do we show that we listen carefully to children and value their contribution?

- Do children appreciate the importance and value of talk in their own learning and treat it with the same significance as their other work?

- Have we drawn up long-term plans for talk, drama, role play?
- Have we planned for a variety of contexts, e.g. pair work, collaborative group work, circle discussions, formal debates, interviews?
- What kinds of purpose for talk have we included across the curriculum?
- Do we plan lessons on oracy in as much detail as other kinds of English work?
- How effectively do we cater for children with special needs, dominant children, shy children, and children who are learning English as an Additional Language?
- Which resources are available and have we exploited them fully?
- How effective are our current attempts to monitor children's progress and attainment in speaking and listening?

A cassette recorder or video can be useful to heighten our awareness of current oracy behaviours in the classroom.

We can use support staff to help us tape or video our own lessons in order to observe our own practice and to:

- analyse the ratio between teacher and pupil talk;
- analyse the kinds of question asked;
- consider whether one group within the class dominates the discourse in any way;
- reflect upon one's own voice and style of interaction as models for the children;
- keep a record of an oracy task, for example, a radio play or jingle, for evaluation later on;
- assess children's contributions individually (e.g. retelling a story) or in small group work, in order to diagnose future learning needs in oracy.

ASSESSMENT

Several chapters of the book contain guidelines for assessment of oracy skills. Structuring our own observations is generally the most systematic and objective way to make judgements about the quality of talk and the levels of pupil achievement. Progress over time is perhaps best charted through our records. Some schools also give each child a cassette which is used to record one or two oral accounts (stories/anecdotes/unscripted descriptions) each academic year.

DIFFERENTIATION

Having identified as accurately as possible children's current levels of achievement, our next step is to identify future individual learning needs. It is important to plan oracy tasks which are achievable by all pupils. It is necessary that we plan differentiation into the lesson. This will mean that:

1. tasks will be matched to a group's or individual's levels of ability and development, involving *differentiation of tasks;*
2. there will be higher or lower levels of support, depending on ability, involving *differentiation of teacher input;*
3. different learning outcomes will be anticipated and accepted, involving *differentiation by outcome.*

HOW TO USE THIS BOOK

Each chapter begins with a Background section, which serves as a brief introduction to its theme. This is followed by a description of the chapter's aims.

There are three main sections in each chapter, **Starting Out**, **Moving On** and **In Full Swing**. These headings suggest that the approaches to oracy described in this book are offered as tentative steps on a longer journey. Nearly all chapters provide examples of oracy work and these are usually identified as Case Studies. Each chapter offers an acrostic reminder of the key points of the chapter.

Finally, there are at least two examples of activity sheets. These are photocopiable pages which are supported by a page of Teachers' Notes. The notes give guidance on how to use, adapt and follow up the exercises on the photocopiable sheets.

Chapter 1

Using Talk Across the Curriculum

Barbara Lalljee

The author has taught in a variety of educational contexts and across the age range. Her main area of work has been within primary schools as teacher, advisory teacher and as co-ordinator on the Oxon-Bucks Oracy Project. More recently she has been working as senior lecturer in the School of Education at Oxford Brookes University. Her areas of expertise lie within the field of Language Development and Psychology of Teaching and Learning.

BACKGROUND

What is talk across the curriculum about? It is about enabling children to use spoken language in a variety of contexts within the classroom environment. It involves giving them the opportunity to extend their vocabulary and their conceptual understanding of words in different subject areas as well as the means to reason and to present information clearly and effectively. This opportunity has to be provided for children at all levels of ability, irrespective of gender and race. The National Curriculum for English sets out specific points regarding range and key skills: these are also highlighted in other Curriculum documents. We are therefore looking at the *process* of using spoken language effectively as well as the *content* of the language used. A particular word may have several meanings in different subject areas. The teacher's task is to make these meanings accessible to the pupils within the classroom and to encourage them to make connections between their learning in different curriculum areas.

The aspects on which I have initially focused are:

1. *The different ways children need to be grouped to extend their language experiences.* Planning for different types of grouping in different curriculum areas is important as pupils frequently work in friendship clusters. These tend to encourage pupils to adopt particular roles or be assigned particular roles by others.

2. *The children's ability to use specific discussion skills.* Different subject areas may require different talking skills, though we should be wary of classifying language use too precisely. In English pupils may narrate a story; in a science experiment they may need to hypothesize or speculate; in maths they may need to problem-solve or argue a particular point of view.

3. *The children's understanding of group dynamics and team work.* In order to work together effectively pupils benefit from being able to talk about appropriate interpersonal and communication skills. Working in groups does not automatically mean working as a team. Team work requires an understanding of how each person in the group can make a contribution or take on a specific role to enable successful completion of a group task. This is a transferable skill which is useful in any subject area.

4. *The children's understanding about speaking and listening skills in different situations outside the school context.* Some pupils come to school with experience of talking to people from different backgrounds, different ages and different cultures. Others may not have had this breadth of experience, so planning for variety is important.

5. *Pupils' ability to use appropriate terminology and vocabulary.* It is important to help pupils refine their language using ever more specific vocabulary within a particular subject in order to communicate with greater clarity and accuracy.

The underlying theme to this chapter is that language, particularly spoken language, is fundamental to learning. This has been acknowledged by psychologists attempting to explain the learning process. A theory of learning put forward by Vygotsky (1978) stated that in order for an individual to learn effectively the learner needs to be in the Zone of Proximal Development – there is the expectation that someone needs to be nearby who understands and is able to support the next step in the learning process. Spoken language is usually the medium through which this support is provided and through which new meanings are then constructed by the learner. Within the educational context it is the teacher, other significant adults, and sometimes peers, who provide this support.

AIMS

The purposes of this chapter are to:

*   show how talk can be effectively incorporated into all curriculum areas for different age groups;

*   highlight the common features of talk in different subjects;

*   emphasize the social aspects of talk so the child is able to develop as an effective speaker *and* listener in different situations and groupings.

Many of the techniques described are widely used (examples are provided in the different chapters of this book). It is their suitable application across the curriculum which is the focus of this chapter.

STARTING OUT

Strategies and techniques

As we use talk across the curriculum, we need to question how we use it and to what effect. Pupils need to develop confidence in using strategies and techniques which are unfamiliar to them. It is the teacher's task to create opportunities for this development by taking into account the different types of talk and by encouraging discussion of how these can be employed in different areas of the curriculum. Very often it is the expectation that all the appropriate skills are acquired within the English curriculum. I would argue that teachers need to plan for spoken language skills in every subject area. To achieve this it is best to work initially in areas of the curriculum in which the teacher feels most confident.

This chapter provides some examples of how teachers use specific talking and listening approaches in different areas of the curriculum.

Things to think about when starting out

The different types of talk

Different curriculum areas require pupils to have the opportunity of using and developing different speaking and listening skills. Do we know whether our pupils are able to do the following – in all or just some subject areas?

announcing	persuading	clarifying	reporting	evaluating	exploring
speculating	instructing	describing	narrating	explaining	criticizing
reflecting	finding out	interpreting	predicting	summarizing	analysing
expressing	presenting	communicating	questioning	comparing	reviewing
demonstrating	investigating	selecting	organizing	problem-solving	responding
arguing a case					

Most of the time we use the above processes without thinking about them, but we need to make these processes explicit in order that we may improve upon them. This requires observation and reflection. It is not possible to observe each and every pupil all of the time, but it is possible to decide which pupils to focus on over the course of a session. For instance, we may want to observe children's ability to analyse a problem: are they speculating, questioning, hypothesizing? On another occasion we may decide to observe the children's ability to communicate: are they describing, explaining, clarifying? Are they using their first language or English?

In setting up such observation schedules it is best to focus on just two or three pupils per session and perhaps to observe these particular pupils using specific skills in different curriculum areas. It is then possible to plan different talk experiences for these pupils. Over a period of time a profile can be developed for each pupil.

The involvement of pupils in the learning process
Pupils can be involved in the planning stages of particular tasks; they can be encouraged to think about the speaking and listening skills involved and about their role in the process. What particular discussion skills are needed in a maths problem-solving task, or in the setting up of a science experiment, or in discussion issues within a story? Are the skills the same in each area or do they require different applications? Both teacher and pupil need to consider the following.

• *Involvement of the children in the planning process:* when we are planning talk activities, what kind of talk are we hoping the children will be involved in? Once we have formulated our plans, the children can become involved. The curriculum does not have to be a guessing game – they can be thinking about starting points for particular activities, posing questions about the subject matter, anticipating different kinds of talk and outcomes and giving consideration to the kind of resources needed to complete a project.

- *Clarity of learning outcomes for particular activities:* are we account of the child's knowledge of talk which he brings to the learning situation? Are we clear about the outcomes we planned for? Are we willing to accept unexpected learning outcomes? Are the pupils able to suggest some possible outcomes?

- *Involvement of children in the evaluation/review process:* do we ask the children to consider whether the task outcomes matched expectations, to analyse the appropriateness of resources or to evaluate their contribution and their learning (with whom and what worked best)?

Allocating pupils into different groupings

I found that children will gravitate to particular groups or partners, and this can be subject-specific. So particular friendship groups will form in PE, or pupils may be ability grouped in maths, given free choice in English, and so on. As the children get older they form closer friendships and tend to want to stay with their friends. It is important to recognize that working mostly with the same people can lead to stereotyping – the pupil who is always the quiet one in a group, the pupil who always takes the lead, the pupil who is seen to be disruptive.

- Children should be given the opportunity to work in friendship groups, but varied groupings provide diverse roles for children so we will be able to observe different aspects of their communication skills, keeping track of who is working with whom and when.

- Changing group size and composition makes it easier to plan for differentiated outcomes for children with varying levels of spoken language experiences.

- Participation in different groups provides children with the opportunity to discuss and understand group dynamics and team work.

Strategies

All of the following strategies can be used in a wide variety of contexts and curriculum areas.

Working in pairs

Pair work builds confidence for the expression of a particular point of view or question. It provides opportunity for thinking things through and for practising what might be said. Through pair work children are generally more motivated to make contributions to class discussion. They begin to appreciate that ideas can be tentative and that discussion can lead them to extend, reject or put ideas 'on ice'. The following is an example from within the English curriculum.

CASE STUDY 1: ENGLISH (POETRY)

Year 1 (6-year-old) children were involved in producing a free form class poem. Choice of topic was reached by brainstorming.

In pairs they talked about their favourite toys (approx. five minutes). Still in pairs they were then encouraged to draw/note/write their ideas on a shared piece of paper (approx. ten minutes). They then regrouped as a class and each pair presented their ideas.

The teacher wrote the ideas as a poem on a large sheet of paper using the children's expressions. The class then read through the 'poem' and talked about any changes the children wanted to make. Finally the poem was made into an illustrated booklet and read with enthusiasm by the children.

Pair work can be planned for in different curriculum areas across the age range. The following are brief examples. It is possible for all of the different types of talk noted earlier to be mapped in at some stage:

Science: Sorting questions in science, formulating hypotheses, planning investigations, discussing and writing up results.

English: Analysing a text, 'critical partners' for editing writing.

Maths: Probing aspects of a problem, listening to each other on 'tables', playing maths games.

Humanities: Analysing historical information, collating data, interviewing informants, reflecting on work achieved.

Art: Discussing ideas, questioning the origin of ideas, evaluating art/craft work.

P.E.:   Discussing proposed work, formulating rules, evaluating work.

As confidence of both teacher and pupils increases, *working in pairs* can be extended across curriculum areas. It is important to keep in mind the type of talking and listening opportunities we could make available to the pupils.

- We need to provide a variety of pairings – always working with the same partner can lead to stereotypical roles.

- We should plan for mixed pairs, same ability, single pairs. Each of these situations will extend our understanding of the pupils' talking and listening skills.

- We need to think about when we are providing opportunities for pair work: at the beginning of a session, during the middle of a session, at the end of a session, or throughout the session. Each of these is a different type of 'talk' situation.

In our record-keeping we need to note who is interacting with whom. This information will be useful for future planning for progress and development (see also Chapter 12).

MOVING ON

Giving speaking and listening space within the curriculum

Brainstorming

It is quite usual to encourage children to make suggestions. The most effective way of doing this is through brainstorming: this can be carried out as a whole class or in small groups (who then pool their ideas).

- Brainstorming means what it says: it allows for *any* idea related to a particular topic or issue to be voiced.

- These suggestions are written on the blackboard/flipchart/whiteboard.

- Only after ideas have been exhausted does the sifting process begin, when impractical or impossible suggestions are eliminated.

- Ideas can then be grouped into areas of investigation.

- This process helps to bring out new ideas and clarify old ones.

A worksheet for sorting ideas after the initial brainstorm is provided (See *Photocopiable Sheet 1:* Brainstorming).

The technique of brainstorming can be used with all age ranges and *in all curriculum areas;* as a starting point to topics; to extend concepts; to reorder thinking.

CASE STUDY 2: HUMANITIES

A class of Year 5/6 (10- to 11-year-old) pupils, was preparing for a visit to Ewelme – a medieval village on the Ridgeway. In order to involve the pupils in the planning process, opportunity was made for a brainstorming session which enabled them to formulate their own questions around the visit.

The pupils were organized into four groups, each group choosing a particular aspect of the village (church, school house, village layout, etc.). They were asked to think about and note down all the different points/questions they might want to find out about.

After this initial brainstorm they shared their ideas with the rest of the class. They were then encouraged to critically look at some teacher-prepared questions, adding these to their own for further discussion if they wished.

All pupils participated in the initial brainstorming.

They felt they could speak with authority about their ideas, having had time to sift, sort and clarify.

The pupils were able to make the content of the visit their own and could then participate in an analytical and evaluative discussion of the teacher-prepared sheet.

Snowballing or Cascading is widely used in non-educational contexts. It is a very useful and effective technique for use in the classroom.

- *Snowballing* involves working in pairs to discuss a problem/topic.
- After five minutes each pair is asked to join up with another pair and to share each other's thoughts on the problem/issue.
- In their fours, the children are asked to distil their ideas and draw up a list.
- Younger children and those not experienced in this process should be asked to list three points. Children with more experience can be asked to list five or more points. With more experience still, the list can be open-ended.
- The points can at this stage be shared with the rest of the class *or*
- fours can become eights, repeating the sharing and distilling process, *and then*
- eights can then share with the rest of the class.

The teacher's role is to monitor and note who is working with whom, observing the patterns of behaviour which may emerge and which need to be considered in forward planning.

CASE STUDY 3: SCIENCE

Snowballing was used very effectively in science with 6-year-olds who were exploring the five senses. Pairs were asked to think about a specific sense and formulate questions to discover how this sense works and is experienced.

Pairs with the same 'sense' (i.e. taste) were then grouped into fours and given time to share their findings. Eventually all ideas were brought back to the whole class, listed on large sheets of paper. These questions and ideas became part of the investigative follow-up work.

All the children became 'expert' in questioning, speculating, theorizing.

Experience in becoming 'expert' empowered children to question others.

Experience in becoming 'expert' provided children with a knowledge base for sharing.

This technique is particularly helpful at the beginning of sessions to 'get the ball rolling' and at the end of sessions to highlight or raise points/questions for evaluation. Young children and children who have not had much experience of this kind of work will improve with practice, so it is important not to give up after the first attempt but to evaluate how the session went, then to remind the children of the important aspects of the process at the beginning of the next session. Photocopiable Sheet 2 could be used here.

Envoying builds on children's experience of working in pairs and small groups. In this situation children have the opportunity to discuss, question, reformulate and clarify issues.

- Children are grouped in fours, sixes or eights, depending on experience of group discussion.

- Each group is allocated a specific aspect relating to a general task.

- The task will vary: it can be to discuss the solution to a problem, to read through a particular piece of evidence and collate points of information, to plan a piece of work.

- The group has to note all relevant points/questions/conclusions that have arisen in relation to the topic/issue.

- After a given amount of time (teacher decision) the children are asked to nominate a representative.

- This representative then visits another group and explains how her/his group reached points/questions/conclusions and invites the new group to help/share in the problem (approx. three to five minutes, depending on complexity of task; it may need more time).

- The representative then returns to the original group and shares comments.

- The group can revise its original plans/conclusions and proceed to implement task.

CASE STUDY 4: PHYSICAL EDUCATION

I felt that my class of 7- to 9-year-olds needed to make their own safety rules for P.E. I had pointed out safety aspects on numerous occasions. I decided to use the envoying technique. I planned for small groups (four to five pupils) and gave each group the task of thinking about safety rules for a specific piece of apparatus. The groups were seated in the hall in a circle. They were allowed ten minutes to brainstorm, discuss and refine their rules, making sure they could back up their rules with reason. Then I asked for a representative from each group to move in a clockwise direction to the next group. When they had joined the next group, they could proceed to share their formulations and invite comment. I allowed five minutes for this task. I then asked the representative to return to their own group and report back to them any comments. Each group was then asked to present its rules to the whole class, noting them on the overhead projector.

Children liked working on P.E. apparatus and were immediately involved in the task. They saw the relevance of the task to their immediate experience. They were able to draw on their knowledge of rules and their experience of working with apparatus. They had the opportunity to share, question, analyse and reason, and so they became expert rule-makers. And they actually adhered to their rules!

Children can develop rules for behaviour in school or classroom, rules for group discussion or activities in the playground.

Envoying is a useful technique when children are trying to sort out problematic aspects of a task. Having the opportunity to formulate their own ideas and raise questions about difficulties, they can then bring these points and queries to others who, with fresh insight, might produce valuable comments which will enable the original group to proceed with their task.

Jigsaw builds on the idea of children as experts. The way it is set up is described on page 17.

Photocopiable Sheet 3: Jigsaw will be found useful in planning and organizing groups. This method of working is applicable to all curriculum areas. It changes the role of the teacher to one of resource person, facilitator, provider of books, materials, etc.

CASE STUDY 5: SCIENCE

This approach was used very effectively by a teacher of Year 7 (12-year-old) pupils in a science project. The children were investigating sources of energy, and their brief was to produce a display and folder highlighting the advantages and disadvantages of different sources of energy. There was total commitment by the children, who chivied those that had not produced the required information to go and get it. The quality of work was very detailed and well executed, and the questions asked at the feedback session demonstrated how deeply the children questioned and probed their own information.

Each child became expert at asking questions, seeking out resources and gathering information.

Each child as expert had the opportunity of contributing and was able to make constructive comments.

Like many of the other techniques, Jigsaw can be used effectively in any of the curriculum areas. It does require careful planning by the teacher to ensure that the children know the aim of the task and are able to follow instructions about the routine.

IN FULL SWING

Building confidence

All the above approaches gradually become part of the classroom routine. I find that as the children become more competent and understand the processes involved, their involvement and motivation improve, as does the quality of their work.

Working with teachers on the Oracy Project highlighted the importance of taking each step slowly, giving time for confidence to build both for the teacher and the pupils, gradually extending the use of a particular approach. As confidence develops so another technique can be introduced. Discussion techniques can complement one another; for instance, brainstorming at the beginning of the session can be followed by envoying to share or clarify ideas while an activity is ongoing.

Examples within this chapter show how the different techniques can be applied to tasks in different curriculum areas. Pupils should be encouraged to discuss how approaches vary depending on the subject area, and how the language they use differs accordingly (i.e. how brainstorming in science might feel different from brainstorming in a poetry session).

It is very important to share experiences of new approaches with other staff in the school. It is helpful for several teachers to introduce the same approach and share their observations and evidence. This enhances mutual understanding of how children progress in their talk across the Curriculum.

A whole-school policy for speaking and listening supports and encourages staff in their attempts to plan for and monitor children's achievements. It can also support teachers' efforts to promote more effectively the status of talk with both children and parents.

The chapters entitled 'Keeping Track of Oracy' and 'Oracy and Children with Special Educational Needs' provide suggestions for further staff development.

KEY POINTS

Children need to be provided with strategies and time for discussion.

Observe and note pupils' use of different strategies.

Meaningful tasks are important for effective discussion.

Make use of pupils' experiences.

Use techniques and skills across the curriculum.

No one should be stereotyped.

Involving the whole school in valuing talk across the curriculum is important.

Creating an effective talk environment needs good planning.

Adapt techniques to different situations.

Talk across curriculum areas develops language skills.

Encourage pupils to discuss their skills.

BRAINSTORMING

Aim: this activity is usually used as a starting point, although it can also be used to generate new thinking or to find solutions to problems, to generate as many ideas as possible, and to organize these ideas for further development.

Objectives:
1. Exploring, developing and clarifying ideas.
2. Predicting outcomes and discussing possibilities.

Group size: small groups/whole class.

Timing: approximately 30 minutes.

Organization: Copy Photocopiable Sheet 1 onto A4 for individual use, but onto A3 for small group use. Hand out sheets and allocate groups. Introduce the class to the concept of brainstorming.

Resources: Photocopiable Sheet 1, pens, pencils.

What to do:
a) Ask the pupils to think of as many ideas about a topic/issue/question as possible (all suggestions are allowed). Example: everything they know about birds. The teacher may act as scribe if it is used as a whole-class activity. Alternatively the pupils can be asked to put their ideas on slips of paper, which are then pinned or 'Blu Tac'-ed on the board. (Timing approx. five minutes.)

b) The next step requires the pupils to find connections between suggestions/ideas and reorganize these. This can be drawn up as a network, flow chart, web, boxes, etc. If slips of paper are used, these can be grouped. Example: all ideas about flight can be grouped together, all ideas about habitat can be grouped together, etc. (Timing approx. ten minutes.)

c) These groups or branches provide the areas for investigation for different groups, pairs or individual pupils. (Timing is dependent on the expected outcomes – report, display, book, etc.)

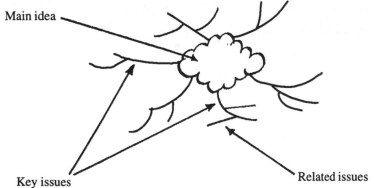

Main idea

Key issues

Related issues

Cross-curricular links: this process can be used in all curriculum areas.

BRAINSTORMING

Write down all ideas/suggestions – use key words rather than sentences.

Now reorganize your ideas into a 'mind map' adding branches or extending branches as needed.

SNOWBALLING

Aims:
1.   To generate as many questions as possible about a topic/issue/problem.
2.   To refine the questioning process.

Objectives: asking and answering questions that clarify understanding.

Group size: whole class, small groups.

Timing: approximately 30 minutes.

Organization: this activity uses the snowballing process (see p. 8). The teacher can model the questioning process. Teacher acts as co-ordinator.

Resources: Photocopiable Sheet 2.

What to do:
The pupils can work in friendship pairs or can be paired off by the teacher. If the pupils work in friendship groups this provides the teacher with the opportunity to observe how they work together, who takes the lead, who makes the most contribution. If pupils are allocated into pairs this can be to give opportunity for working in mixed pairs, single sex pairs, pairing two dominant children, two quiet children. Merging pairs can again take these characteristics into account.

1.   In pairs, pupils are either provided with a topic/issue/problem or choose one.
2.   They try and generate as many questions as possible. A time limit should be imposed, but different topics require different 'gestation' periods. When generating questions it is advisable to allow time for discussion and development. (An alternative is to specify the number of questions. This is useful when pupils are new to this type of work.)
3.   The pupils list the questions on the photocopies.
4.   When the time limit has been reached, the pupils are asked to move into fours (or are allocated into fours by the teacher). At this stage they are asked to share their questions and write down any new ones they generate. Again, it is advisable to put a time limit on the task (approximately ten minutes).
5.   a) The pupils can now proceed with finding the answers to the questions generated.
      b) The pupils can share their questions with the whole class. This usually elicits quite interesting discussions around the fact that many of the questions might be similar. Also this is the time when thinking has been stimulated and new questions may be forthcoming.

Cross-curricular links: this activity can be used in all curriculum areas.

Photocopiable Sheet 2

SNOWBALLING

Name of topic:

Names of pair A: _____ and _____ .

Names of pair B: _____ and _____ .

1.   In pairs, list all the possible questions you could ask about the topic.

*   _____

*   _____

*   _____

*   _____

*   _____

2.   Now working in fours, share your questions and write down any new ones you think
     will be interesting.

*   _____

*   _____

*   _____

*   _____

*   _____

3.   At this stage you may be asked to share all your questions with the whole class. Which
     questions did you find the most interesting and why?

     [ ]   because _____

     [ ]   because _____

     [ ]   because _____

Teachers' Notes 3

JIGSAW

Aims:
1. To enable pupils to become 'expert' in an aspect of a particular project.
2. To provide pupils with the experience of working in different groupings.
3. To give every pupil the opportunity to make a contribution.

Objectives:
1. Describing events, observations and experiences.
2. Making simple, clear explanation of choices.

Group size: this is a whole-class activity.

Timing: this activity can take from half an hour to several sessions.

Organization: a topic or project can be chosen from different areas of the curriculum e.g. energy (science), a visit (geography, history), etc. A decision needs to be made about the sub-categories – this can be made by the teacher or the pupils using the brainstorming technique. Once the subcategories have been defined, it is possible to arrange the Jigsaw. For instance, energy can be subdivided into different types of power: solar, coal, water. The subcategories dictate the number of expert groups. The size of the class dictates the number of home groups, e.g. if there are four subcategories and 32 children in the class, there will be eight home groups with four experts in each. A further decision has to be made as to the type of outcome that is expected of each home group's project: the outcome may be a display, a report, a presentation, etc. At this stage it is necessary to decide the size of the home group and who will be in each one.

Resources: Photocopiable Sheet 3, pens, pencils.

What to do:
1. The class will be divided into equal-sized groups. These are called home groups.
2. Each group has to complete a project – this could be writing a story, producing a poster, writing an article. In order to do this they have to collect all the relevant information.
3. The home group discusses the different aspects, resources, etc. needed to complete the task.
4. The group numbers off one to four (or however many there are). Then all the number ones meet up, all the number twos meet up, and so on.
5. Each new group then becomes expert at a particular aspect which they investigate as fully as possible. For example, the Ones will look at solar energy, the Twos at water power, the Threes fossil power, the Fours wind power.
6. Each group member has to make notes, gather information and fully participate because they will have to bring their information back to the home group.
7. After a given amount of time home groups regroup and each member is given the opportunity to report back all their findings. If a member has not fully participated, the group task as a whole will suffer. (When children first experience this way of working this may happen. They very quickly learn how to become fully effective.)
8. Each group then presents its completed folder/report/display/story and invites comments from the other members of the class.

Cross-curricular links: science, maths, geography.

Photocopiable Sheet 3

JIGSAW

This sheet can be adapted as required.

Home groups:

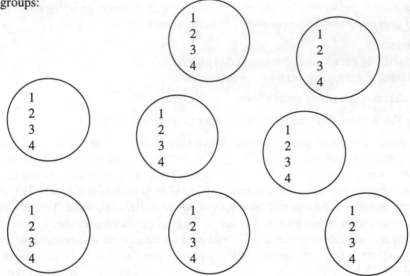

Expert groups:

1	2	3	4
1	2	3	4
1	2	3	4
1	2	3	4
1	2	3	4
1	2	3	4
1	2	3	4
1	2	3	4

Chapter 2

Play and Inventive Activity

Bill Laar

Bill Laar has been a primary headteacher, an adviser and inspector for several local authorities, including ILEA, and an educational consultant and author. Until recently, he was Chief Inspector for Westminster City Council. He is a Registered OFSTED inspector and writes and lectures widely on education. He is currently co-director of an Early Years Project, which focuses on home-school liaison, literacy partnerships and the role of play in learning.

BACKGROUND

Children learn primarily because they want to find out about their environment and to make sense of what is happening in their lives. Oral language is central to this process. It enables children to communicate, to ask questions, to try out their opinions and viewpoints on others, to express wishes and feelings, to form hypotheses and to analyse and reflect on their experience. We can deduce from this that oral language is acquired by young children as much through their own active learning, as by it being taught to them in any strictly formal sense.

For young children in the early stages of cognitive development, play and what I call 'inventive activity' are probably the most powerful forms of such active learning. Language development and oracy skills are, by implication, strongly related to play and dependent on it to a significant degree.

It is essential therefore for schools to provide for play as a major component of children's education prior to and throughout Key Stage 1 and indeed, in certain forms, into Key Stage 2.

AIMS

This chapter will be concerned with how schools can provide for various forms of play and, through it, for the development of oracy. We shall consider the following matters:

- play as an agent of learning, with some practical illustrations of this;
- the links between play and language development;
- baseline assessment of children's competence in oracy;
- how play can be organized in terms of resources, time and space;
- the role of the teacher as organizer and provider, and the extent to which she/he should intervene;
- assessment and recording.

The aims of play

Schools provide for play for a variety of reasons. In general, however, they seek to:

- provide rich experience which naturally challenges and encourages children to be active learners;
- extend children's existing knowledge, experience and understanding, to practise and consolidate their learning, and to structure opportunities for the development of individual competences;
- encourage children to apply what they already know, and have learned, to the solution of problems;
- enable children to explore and discover, to experiment, reflect on and draw conclusions from what they have done, to investigate the properties and functions of materials, implements and artefacts, and to choose and use them for their appropriate purpose;
- promote children's emotional, physical, cultural and social development;
- cultivate independent behaviour and autonomous learning, promote self-reliance and the capacity for decision-making, the ability to plan, organize and complete projects;
- enable children to socialize and form relationships, to work and co-operate with others, to appreciate and respect others people's rights and

qualities, to understand the need for fair play, to express feelings and needs;

- develop the imagination, the capacity to fantasize, to be inventive, to engage in pretence and role play;
- promote language development and especially oracy, including the ability to:
  - recall, describe and report on events and experience; to retell stories, summarize conversation, describe pictures, recount events in sequence;
  - extend vocabulary;
  - make personal needs, purposes, intentions, perceptions clear, pose relevant questions, express feelings and responses;
  - ask for information and guidance;
  - give directions and instructions; use language to organize;
  - maintain and justify action, and clarify roles;
  - monitor, direct and maintain personal actions, work and behaviour;
  - predict what will happen in particular circumstances and as an outcome of actions;
  - project into the future, speculate and hypothesize;
  - describe the characteristics and attributes of objects and compare things by size, shape, colour and position.

Young children learn through being problem-solvers. From the beginning they investigate the puzzling and the unknown to discover how they work and what they mean. They experiment with all the things that make up their environment. They use all their senses to acquire and practise important skills. They strive to understand how it is that other people behave as they do. They try to come to terms with emotions and relationships. Case Studies 1, 2 and 3 provide some evidence of this.

Play and language are the main agents in this learning process. Play that is well planned and pleasurable helps children to think. Through play they increase their understanding and improve their language competence. Play allows children to explore and investigate their surroundings, to experiment and test their conclusions. Play is where imagination and work meet.

It is adults who tend to confuse children's play with leisure and who draw a distinction between play and work. For children, play is analogous to the work of the scientist, the gardener, the builder and the artist. Play is as serious in purpose, as demanding in terms of intellectual effort and concentration, as potentially frustrating and full of pitfalls as the work and study of adults.

CASE STUDY 1: PLASTERING

Some children who had been watching with great interest a workman plastering in the school, began 'plastering' an exterior wall using improvised tools and sand and water. They represented the hods and trowels with some accuracy but became frustrated by the fact that their mixture of sand and water did not adhere to the wall. At the teacher's request they talked with the workmen who explained how the plaster was constituted and allowed them to 'plaster' a large piece of hardboard.

CASE STUDY 2: FILMING

A group of children who had seen an advertising film being made in a garage across the way from the school began making their own film about a horse race (inspired by the Grand National on television) over 'hurdles' erected in the playground. At first they were satisfied merely to gallop round the track, and indeed the 'camera man' simulated the filming with a 'box' camera as if taking still photographs. Gradually however, entirely at the children's instigation, and with the teacher intervening only in response to requests for technical assistance with equipment, 'proper' TV cameras were constructed and operated from a rostrum, there was a starting tape, a race commentator, an ambulance and stretcher bearers.

CASE STUDY 3: GARDENING

A group of children who had been watching the school-keeper water, with considerable difficulty, flowers on a high bank in the school garden, played at gardening in the sand pit outside their classroom. At first they were content to 'plant' the flowers and water them liberally with improvised watering cans. Then, however, they constructed a bank similar to the one in which the school-keeper had been engaged, but instead of using the can to water in the normal way, they constructed irrigation channels from the top of the bank, to avoid the difficulties he had encountered.

Play is serious business for children. Most play makes demands upon them. To achieve what they want to do they are likely to have to do some planning, to identify what they will need, to have an order of priority, to decide upon materials, to find objects that will substitute for or be equivalent to others, to organize other children, to explain what it is they want to do, to negotiate, persuade, bargain, allocate roles and organize proceedings. In the process they

come to understand the need for interpersonal skills and co-operation, th
that people have personal desires and intentions that call for understar
acceptance and accommodation. They learn about leadership, about co-operation, about contributing to a corporate effort. They are obliged to articulate
their needs and intentions, to question, explain, give instructions, offer
approval and advice. They learn how to win the interest and involvement of
adults when it is required.

Play is heavily dependent upon language for its power as a learning tool.
Language, and especially talk, are central to the process of learning. We know
from research and from the constant observations of teachers and carers that
language enables the learner to question, analyse, reflect upon, review and
come to an understanding of phenomena and events, helps to make experience meaningful, and translate what is thought into expression. Oral language
is a component of our thinking. Language and intellectual growth are insepa-
rable, and cyclically dependent upon each other, with growth in one
promoting growth in the other. Processes of investigation, experimentation
and enquiry call for various forms of discourse: interrogation, dialogue,
description and argument.

There are fewer places where this is more clearly illustrated than in the
interdependence of play and talk. A very young child who totters round in her
mother's shoes, draped in scarves, weighed down by a handbag or briefcase
is obviously engaged in play. In fact she is also working out purposeful adult
behaviour, preparing to go to the office, of whose purpose she is still wholly
ignorant. She accompanies her actions with words that state and reinforce
what she already knows, and that question and seek further information. Her
store of language and her vocabulary are likely to be augmented and amend-
ed as she shares the play with adults.

This is not to assume there is unanimity among educationists about the
purpose of play and how it should be provided for. There are those who argue
that play is essentially child-centred, that it is concerted with child development, with affective and emotional growth, generated out of the needs,
instincts, wishes and exploration of children. Any formal structuring of the
play by adults is regarded as inhibiting and counter-productive. The adult's
role is to be a catalyst where appropriate. However, it is generally accepted
that it is essentially through play that children begin to acquire and develop
important skills, concepts and understanding.

As will be seen from examples throughout this chapter, this process
involves in almost every case the use of language in one form or another.
Children will ask questions, make suggestions, and comparisons, put forward
theories, ideas and tentative hypotheses, will offer reasons and justification

for actions; even when playing alone children will often steer, monitor and provide encouragement for themselves, will talk their way step by step through a sequence of events, will reflect on developments, will express pleasure, relief, exasperation, will predict how their games and activities are going to turn out.

We are left therefore with a kind of developmental loop:

*   young children learn because they want to make sense of things;
*   in the early stages of their lives one of the most natural and obvious ways to do this is through play, a much more serious and complex process than may appear on the surface;
*   play usually requires language to take it forward;
*   the more varied the play, the more challenging the situation, the wider the collaboration with others, then the more diverse and developed will be the language that is generated.

STARTING OUT

Management and organization

This complex process does not occur by chance. Children of course have the capacity to play with remarkable perseverance in the most limited and unpromising situations, with the minimum of materials. Most people will be familiar with situations where children denied access to sophisticated toys will become absorbed in playing, often very inventively, with the boxes that contain them. Even out of the most apparently limited play some language, however slight, is likely to come. For example, a child spent prolonged periods dragging behind her a box which substituted for the dog she was to receive for her birthday and which she trained to 'obey' a series of commands, including a 'highway code for dogs' which she herself devised.

But play, if it is to contribute systematically to the development of essential and complex language competences and if it is to be a means of responding to and further developing ideas, must be carefully planned and richly and sensitively provided for. Some teachers will object that adult 'manipulation' negates the true nature and purpose of play, channelling it in artificial directions, and robbing the play of vital spontaneity.

However, it is more likely that play that is ill provided for, and deprived of the stimulus of adult interest and participation, will often exhaust itself without generating genuine learning and language development. On the other hand, where adults plan for development and progression, participate when invited to, or when they judge it likely to be helpful, and sensitively move matters forward through questions, suggestions and advice, helping children to focus on fresh dimensions and challenges, then the potential for language development will be greatly increased.

CASE STUDY 4: PLAY SITUATION

A good example of this is provided by a play situation involving infants who were very excited by the arrival of a fairground on the common near the school. The way in which the teacher became involved in the process provides an insight into the way many teachers manage the organization of play and the time allocated to it. Having decided that the interest aroused by the specific theme was likely to lead to productive play and learning, she intervened in specific ways and devoted considerable time to the project.

There was initially a whole-class discussion in which the teacher led the children to describe their experiences and recollections of a fair, the turns and activities they preferred, and to make comparisons with pleasure parks they had visited. They were anxious to set up a fair. The teacher encouraged them to select the essential elements of the fair that could be realistically set up. During the debate one child suggested they should first make a model of the fairground which she claimed would make the real one easier to plan. When the suggestion failed to gain support she went off and began independently to construct a model from card. Some children's interest did not survive the discussion and they drifted away to other activities, while the others split up into groups to concentrate on a particular aspect:

- two children became absorbed in preparing their baby and the pram to visit the fair, with clothing, various food and drink provision and an 'anti-kidnap' alarm;
- a group set up dodgems using many of the wheeled toys from the outside play area;
- a group organized a noisy shooting range;
- two children invited a helper to join them in making a fortune-telling booth;
- a group spent the morning simulating situations that involved manoeuvring 'turns' into position and setting up the various stalls and side-shows. This group sought out the girl who was making the fairground model for consultation about the range of activities.

The following forms of conversation arose from the different groups:

- children expressed intentions and wishes, and described how they would carry out plans and what their activity would look like;
- they advanced arguments for their type of fairground;

- they gave directions, advice and instructions and allocated tasks;
- they described how particular materials would be necessary to create parts of the fairground.

The teacher provided direct advice and encouragement at the beginning, supporting with ideas and suggestions, involving the whole class and allocating the morning discussion period to the topic. However as soon as individuals, pairs or groups began to break away and pursue their own interests – for example, the child making the model, and the baby minders – she allowed them to do so. She later provided practical support for the model-maker. She intervened with the dodgems, shooting range and fairground helpers groups, merely to temper noisy and more boisterous activities and to ensure the play was safely carried out. (In fact the shooting range and the dodgems continued for a few days, intermittently, before the children exhausted their possibilities.) In both cases the teacher spent a few minutes each day discussing what they were doing, allowing them to play for some time before requiring them to be involved in other learning activities.

She intervened much more directly with selected groups where she felt there was potential in their activities for learning and language development, but where sustained support was needed if interesting ideas, suggestions and intentions were not to be frustrated. Using a flipchart to write down their various suggestions, the teacher then helped them to prioritize, to decide what was realistic, to adapt ideas rather than merely discard them, to itemize the materials and indicate the space they would require and to allocate roles and responsibilities.

This is a good example of a situation rooted in children's interest and excitement about an experience that many of them had shared, that was subsequently influenced and, to an extent, directed by the teacher to achieve particular learning purposes: problem-solving, large-scale construction, technology, collaborative planning and, of course, language development. She felt that the language outcomes alone justified the structuring she had imposed. The following language activities were noted. The children:

- participated as speakers and listeners in a group engaged in a given task;
- described a real event;
- responded appropriately to simple and more complex instructions;
- listened with an increased span of concentration to other children and adults;
- gave, received and followed precise instructions.

All these language features are part of the National Curriculum for Speaking and Listening.

For some teachers such a development would no longer constitute play, because of the extent of the teacher's intervention. They would regard the play as no longer authentic and therefore unlikely to be valuable once the children became, in any sense, reluctant or unsure about further engagement in it. While quite willing to acknowledge the value of the collaboration and language development resulting from the teacher's intervention, they would be more concerned to preserve the play and allow the children to decide when they had exhausted it. Most primary teachers, however, not only regard play as an important part of children's learning, but view such organization, structure and adult intervention as essential, if its true value in learning terms is to be realized. This is largely due to the circumstances in which teachers work. They are, after all, required to deliver a prescribed and extensive curriculum to large classes, are frequently restricted in terms of space and resources, and are faced with high expectations from parents, colleagues and inspectors about what will be achieved. They feel they must justify the place of play by demonstrating very clearly how it contributes to learning and language development, especially as children mature. They are reluctant to accept that this is likely to happen without close attention and detailed planning, without consideration of play in relation to the whole curriculum, and the most productive ways in which teachers and adults can intervene and contribute.

There are two matters to be borne in mind before we consider how these vital elements can be managed and organized, and how environments, resources, time and space can be provided to ensure productive play. They are these:

1. Teachers need to have a clear picture of where children 'are at' in terms of cognitive and motor development, what their 'existing knowledge, understanding and skills are' and the implications of that for their learning. Teachers can begin to construct a map of children's development based on some of the following criteria:

    *   Amount of help required in classroom, extent of concentration, capacity to play alone and with others, muscle and motor control.

    *   Competence in construction tasks, cutting shapes, control of pencil, ability to use brushes, to sort familiar objects according to criteria, to count, match and sequence objects, to walk, run, skip confidently, to pedal and steer a bike, to draw circles, squares, triangles, to build a small tower of bricks, to match shapes and pictures, to recognize the first letter of their name, to draw and paint using different materials, draw a simple human figure, to copy adult writing, and to invite adults to write things down.

2.   Teachers must strive to be as fully informed as possible about stages of language development and progression and be able to identify children's competence in terms of spoken language. They must understand how children can be enabled to reflect on their use of language, to appreciate what they are achieving through the use of language, to be conscious of their developing control and competence.

Teachers can begin to chart the stages of children's language development by finding out through direct observation and detailed discussion with parents and carers about children's interests, experience, skills, attitudes and knowledge. They can begin to observe, record and monitor the following:

- what they can say about play and the things they like to do;

- whether they can make themselves understood;

- whether they know nursery rhymes, look at books, have favourite stories, follow print, pretend to read;

- their willingness to speak in school, with friends, in group situations, with the teacher;

- whether they use single words, phrases or sentences when describing something that is important to them;

- whether they can use language to secure the co-operation of others, to indicate they want to take part, to negotiate a position for themselves, to contribute to planning, to express personal opinions, to reason about things;

- their ability to give instructions, advice, comfort or directions;

- their use of adjectives to describe objects or to describe the day's weather;

- their use of language to maintain position, e.g. we can see the wide development from the child doggedly but narrowly arguing his right to next turn with the scooter to the girl who establishes her right to be hospital doctor on the grounds that she originally suggested the theme.

These complex linguistic skills range across an extended continuum. In the case of using language to maintain social position for example, we can see a continuum of development from the child doggedly arguing his right to the next turn with the scooter, to the child who establishes her right to be doctor because she originally suggested the hospital theme. The teacher's task is to identify where precisely a child is on such a continuum and to decide how play and other learning situations can take that skill a stage further.

Progress in speaking and listening is characterized by increasing:

- clarity, fluency and confidence of thought and expression;
- vocabulary; comprehension of what is heard;
- proficiency in different kinds of talk; ability to sustain an explanation or description; ability to listen with concentration to more complex and varied speech.

The teacher's task is to track children's competence in oracy, supported by reference to the National Curriculum Programme of Study for Speaking and Listening.

Resources

People increasingly recognize that from the moment of birth – many would suggest that even through the period of gestation – children require stimulus that will arouse curiosity, excite and extend interest, challenge the imagination, encourage thinking, provide pleasure and aesthetic fulfilment. Parents are increasingly encouraged by the commercial world to make such provision. It is imperative that schools continue and extend such provision, especially in areas beyond the resources of the home.

Teachers have to build into children's experience certain stimuli that, in addition to their own intrinsic value, suggest and foster different modes of play. Such stimuli include: pictures and story books of all kinds, walks, outings and expeditions, opportunity to grow things and keep small creatures, access to an attractive outside environment with large games and activities, a diversity of games and puzzles, judicious use of films, video and TV, and some, at least, of the range of materials described below. This, of course, is an ideal list, and much of it may not be immediately available to teachers. Even if it were, it would need to be used selectively and carefully. Some materials will be constantly required by children, some will be made available by teachers at specific times to suggest or stimulate particular developments and some will emerge in response to a particular requirement.

RESOURCES FOR DOMESTIC PLAY

House furniture, much of it improvised from large boxes and containers.

Telephones, including portable and answer-phones.

Writing equipment found in the home, e.g. computer, message pads, shopping lists.

Equipment for maintaining the household, e.g. cleaning materials, tea towels, mops.

Do-It-Yourself equipment and gardening equipment, e.g. tool kit, wheelbarrow.

Adult-sized utensils including cutlery and crockery, candlesticks, etc.

Condiments, spices and food packets, containers and jars.

Bathroom furnishings and equipment, e.g. bath toys, toiletries, mirrors.

Dressing-up clothes and equipment to suit a range of occupations, professions, fantasy and fairytale and story roles, e.g. jewellery and accessories.

A wide range of fabrics that can be used for improvisation.

A variety of dolls, male and female from various ethnic backgrounds together with a range of doll's clothing.

RESOURCES FOR CONSTRUCTIVE PLAY

Variously sized bricks and blocks.

Boards, barrels, tubs, lengths of wood, ramps, a wide variety of cardboard boxes.

Layouts: train and track sets, harbour, farm, racetrack and building site, fort and castle.

Dolls' houses and contents.

Miniature cars, motor bikes, buses, coaches, lorries, pick-up trucks, fire engines, ambulances, cranes.

Construction kit equipment: e.g. Mobilo, Duplo, Lego etc.

Construction and building are likely to require string, pulleys, Sellotape, masking tape, white glue, newsprint, staples, staplers, perhaps nails, woodwork tools, paste, paperclips, elastic, rubber bands, wire, needles, thread.

Model-making will require modelling clay, play-dough, rolling pins, plastic knives, cutters, straws, buttons, cotton reels, various wood pieces, including balsa, paper bags, stockings, tights, shirts, all kinds of cloth and fabrics, felt, leather, suede, velvet, sequins, cardboard, tubing.

RESOURCES FOR SAND AND WATER PLAY

Pans, dishes, all kinds of cartons, squeeze and plastic bottles, spoons, shovels, scoops, plastic cars, trucks, cranes, yachts, plastic boats, tin cans, tubing, buckets, spades, plastic measures, moulds, sand wheels, sand mills, wheelbarrow, watering cans, paddle-boats, water pumps, sieves, water-play table, large sand trays.

RESOURCES FOR SORTING AND BUILDING

Sequencing beads, strings, pegs, pegboards, cubes, attribute blocks, stones, marbles, buttons, shells, nesting boxes, cups and rings, plastic piping, washers, nuts, bolts.

RESOURCES FOR MAKE-BELIEVE AND CREATIVE PLAY

Junk material: foil, doilies, paper plates, all kinds of cardboard, wallpaper, egg cartons, ice-cream tubs and food cartons and containers, boxes, pipe cleaners, cardboard rolls and tubing, ribbon, wood off-cuts, string, rope, straws, lollipop sticks, beads, sequins, pieces of fabric, carpet squares, leather, fur, suede, curtain rings, corks, netting, gauze, canes.

Printed material: newspapers, magazines, catalogues, calendars, address books, tickets, receipts, posters, diaries.

Puppets: paper bags, string, gloves, masks.

Dressing-up clothes and accessories, e.g. binoculars, old watches.

CASE STUDY 5: A PUPPET PLAY

Three children made simple cardboard cut-out figures for a puppet play based on the episode from 'The Little Toy Soldier' in which the hero is put in a paper boat by two boys and sent floating down the gutter. This play was initiated and carried through by the children without any adult involvement, save for the teacher's observation of the children's talk. This took the form of directing and advising each other about the construction of the puppets and speculation as to how they would operate them. The children reflected back on the place of the episode in the whole story, planned how the episode would be presented to other children, and decided it would be a trial for other episodes. In fact following a 'showing' to a small group there were no further episodes; these able children showed no interest in taking the matter further, but the teacher noted evidence of growing competence in specific areas of oracy on which further development could be planned.

RESOURCES FOR OUTDOOR PLAY

Large cardboard boxes, containers for fridges, TV sets, washing machines and deep freeze units, work benches with vices and tools, crates, barrels, tree trunks, hammocks, ramps, slides, drainage pipes, tents, tyres, inner tubes, paddling pools, sand pits, mattresses, ropes, trampolines, climbing frames and jungle gyms, mats.

Space

Discussion of resources leads us naturally to the issue of space, one of the major challenges for teachers in providing for play. Teachers will want to enable children to engage in domestic, construction, exploratory, make-believe, imaginative and fantastic play, to play individually, in small and large groups, and to use the outside environment.

How is space to be provided for all this? For example, to provide for hospital play alone, one of the most natural and common forms of play experienced by children in school could well exhaust all the classroom space available to a teacher and mean that that particular form of play – not necessarily enticing for all children – is all that is available for some time. The following strategies will help:

- Efficient and economic storage of materials: store all small, loose items, whether they be pencils, crayons, felt-tip pens or sorting and small building materials, in large plastic or fabric pockets suitable for hanging on the backs of cupboards and open shelving. Store other small materials in plastic tubs and trays that can be placed on top of each other, separated by wooden boards. Hang pots, pans and other utensils from hooks. Use clothes lines and trellis to provide space to display children's paintings, and for interactive displays. A coat-rack prevents dressing-up clothes from becoming wrinkled and unattractive.

- All containers need to be clearly labelled, with a picture and name so that children become familiar with the location of materials. It is essential that children are trained to clear away and store materials and equipment properly, and to be able to distribute them efficiently. When there are clear routines for storage, when children understand their vital role in taking out and putting away (teachers will be aware of the learning inherent in such disciplined and ordered activities) and are trained to carry them out responsibly and systematically, then there is much less likely to be the clutter and disorganization that reduce available space.

- There may be occasions when some space is available in corridors or cloak rooms, where certain kinds of play provision can be located and carried on without undue disruption for the rest of the class, e.g. big bricks and building materials, sand and water play, dressing-up and make-believe play. Occasionally the hall, or at least part of it, may be used for some forms of play and, of course, if outside space is available, then play with scooters, trucks, cars, large toys, woodwork benches, sand and water play, climbing, swinging and jumping activities can be located there.

- Some play equipment will stay out semi-permanently, while a particular topic or interest is being pursued: sand, water, sawdust, clay, dressing-up clothes will be so commonly used that they are likely to retain much the same positions, but a whole range of toys, of small world equipment, utensils and containers may need to be packed away daily when play is over.

Time

The question of time allocation is probably even more problematic and certainly less clear-cut than providing resources and space. Much will depend upon school philosophy and policy and upon the extent to which play is perceived as a major source of learning and, of course, upon the attitude of individual teachers. Teachers may allocate time in the following ways:

- much of the day's work is based upon play activities (usually with very young children) with such activities frequently serving as a starting-point for further various kinds of learning;
- part of the day, especially at the beginning and end, or when children have completed particular set assignments or activities, is allocated to play;
- a particular proportion of the week, perhaps half a day, is set aside specifically for play purposes.

It is easy of course to be critical of what may be seen as a rather mechanistic allocation of time, with children almost 'directed' in the way they play. However, it has to be borne in mind that many schools and teachers who readily accept the value of play feel increasingly compelled from the beginning of the reception stage to implement the detailed and demanding National Curriculum requirements. As a result they feel obliged to curtail the time devoted to play, and where it is implemented, feel that it must be seen to contribute to learning and achievement in the core curriculum.

MOVING ON

Teacher intervention in play

When and how, then, should teachers intervene in children's play? Teachers will intervene for some or all of the following reasons:

- to bring about particular developments in the play so that the full potential learning inherent in a situation is realized;

- to encourage children to bring to and utilize in their play the skills they are already acquiring; for example, the ability to plan and organize.
- to support children who may be diffident about becoming fully involved in play;
- to use play in ways that will help children to acquire new skills or to extend their awareness and knowledge;
- to integrate play with other learning activities.

Teacher intervention will take the form of helping children to explore materials, to adapt and improvize them, to call upon experience, knowledge and awareness of books, story and TV to enrich the play, and to foster discussion, language exchange, the development of new forms and vocabulary. They will make suggestions about how situations can be developed and how tools, equipment and toys might be used. They will take forward faltering but interesting development, will move play away from the possibility of becoming routine and settling in a groove and will constantly seek opportunity to extend and develop the language competences referred to throughout the chapter.

CASE STUDY 6: AN EXCURSION TO THE SEASIDE

This involved an entire nursery school, all the staff and a large number of parents. The whole enterprise took place at school, but was planned and carried through as if the excursion was genuine. All the necessary equipment – bathing costumes, towels, carrier bags, sun glasses, binoculars, picnics in hampers, fishing-rods, toy boats and yachts, lilos, buckets and spades – was prepared.

The children boarded the 'coach' and had a sing-song and a refreshment break before arriving at the 'seaside' in the playground area. Here there were ice-cream stalls, fish-and-chip shops, sand, a cave, rowing boats and so on. The children paddled, swam, explored the cave, had a barbecue and picnic, went to the fairground and played games. This was obviously a 'one-off' enterprise by a highly imaginative staff, supported by enthusiastic parents who invested considerable effort to simulate all the exciting events of an excursion.

Before the 'outing' the children talked about their previous experience of the seaside, and indicated what they would do when they arrived. They talked about personal intentions, hazards that might be encountered, how much money would be needed, and what food would be required. They drew up detailed lists of equipment for the expedition and selected partners and supervisors, and rehearsed songs for the coach journey.

The coach journey inspired new vocabulary and language forms, as did the carefully organized events at the seaside, including the feeling of walking in sand, paddling in rock pools, jumping up and down among the waves, rowing boats and going to the fun-fair.

IN FULL SWING

Teacher intervention

Effective play therefore is dependent upon a school philosophy and a practical policy, upon a clear understanding by teachers of its place and value, and upon adequate resourcing, time and space. In practical terms play may vary greatly from school to school. Unlike other curriculum areas the time devoted to it will decline rather than increase as children mature and develop. The following examples show us play and inventive activity in 'full swing', but in very diverse ways. In all cases teachers intervene to structure the play so that individual developmental needs are met and language competence is fostered.

CASE STUDY 7: RESTORATION

Reception children had been intrigued by extensive restoration of a nearby large house and garden, which some of them regarded as a 'vampire's house'. They brought in daily reports of the progress made and had played out some of the building restoration. The teacher felt that this was a situation that could be taken further, for a number of reasons. The children were already devising play situations relating to the house, and although these often ran out of inspiration fairly quickly, the children frequently returned to them.

The restoration was likely to go on for some time and to continue to stimulate the children's curiosity. It was diverse work including garden landscaping, the replacement of part of the roof and windows, the laying down of a new drive and external painting. Materials were constantly being delivered. The teacher was sure the situation offered the potential for various forms of language development, provided that some structure was introduced and particular resources were available. She was anxious at the same time to allow the children's interest and curiosity to determine the outcome. She therefore took the following steps:

- arranged a walk to the house to enable all the children to have a good view of the wide range of activities;
- had a discussion on their return to clarify exactly what was taking place;
- talked about the materials that were being used, and introduced proper names and terminology.
- persuaded the children to talk about particular aspects that interested them and how they would go about these, which implements they would use and in what ways.

She talked about how they might simulate materials and implements. A range of language emerged from the discussion. Children described what they had seen, what they thought was happening, how a concrete- mixer worked, why some of the workers wore masks, why some trees were cut down while others were allowed to survive, why a tunnel was used to carry away debris, why a hedge was being replaced by a brick wall, how the bricklayers worked, how skips could be moved, why windows had to be replaced. Discussions ranged round the different types of machines and materials – asphalt, concrete, cement – and the various tools being used. There was particular debate about the importance of different jobs, arising from the fact that one parent was a carpenter and another a painter and decorator.

The teacher left the matter there, making no suggestions initially as to how, or indeed whether, the children should take things further. However, some of the children became engaged in more long-term play based upon elements of the work.

1.   A tarmacadam group used trolleys and other wheeled containers to simulate mechanical spreaders, wore Wellington boots, aprons and goggles, had a member of the group operate a 'stop-go' board for traffic.
2.   A second group made windows and rigged up a rope and pulley on the hall wall-bars to put the windows in place.
3.   A third group used boxes and planks to set up 'scaffolding' from which they 'picked' the walls, replastered and then painted them.

The teacher described a wide range of conversation between the children:

- new vocabulary was discovered and used to describe, explain, clarify and give instructions and orders;
- language was used to secure the co-operation of others, to contribute to planning and to organize activities, to explain technical terms, to explain to others what they knew from personal experience, for example, about particular trades and jobs;
- opinions were expressed and positions and tasks were negotiated;
- language was used to suggest how particular materials and artefacts could be improvized and adapted to stand for essential tools and equipment;
- fantastic and imaginative stories were invented about the house;
- groups responded to invitations to describe to others what their activities were about.

There are certain points worth noting about this example:

- a large degree of choice was left to the children, and considerable elements of pure play survived. The teacher was anxious to maintain the play experience;
- the teacher's intervention was largely about the structuring of opportunity, e.g. arranging the walk, the provision of materials, advice and suggestions where needed;
- crucially, however, she continued to observe and to intervene, however slightly, to nurture conversation, debate and discussion;
- she recorded what she regarded as significant language developments.

Assessing and recording play

A main characteristic of play is its random and unpredictable nature. It may exhaust itself almost as soon as commenced, or continue intermittently over a period of days; it may involve one, a few, or several children, is likely to develop in a variety of ways, and generate ranges of language not always heard by adults.

CASE STUDY 8: AN ORPHANAGE

A group of children, inspired by TV news and actively supported by a classroom helper, turned the home corner into an orphanage for war refugees. Their extensive preparations to receive the orphans included the provision of an 'interpreter'. This element was introduced by the helper who asked how they would deal with children who spoke no English, and helped them to reflect on how the issue was dealt with in their own multi-ethnic school.

This piece of play involved the children in significant consideration of the purpose of language and why it is essential to communication.

If play is to be fully exploited for learning and language development then teachers need to systematically record and assess what is taking place as a basis for further development. They will find it helpful to record the following:

- the nature of the play, length of time occupied, numbers of children involved;
- what gave rise to the play;
- any problems raised by the play and solved by the children;
- materials used and space occupied;
- the different forms of conversation and talk used;
- progress by individual children in relation to specific language forms.

Such assessment will provide not only an indication of children's oral development but an evaluation of the provision for play and the effectiveness of the teacher's intervention. The examples of play that have been considered suggest the following:

- play is natural for young children and takes place in a variety of circumstances;
- play is central to children's learning and language development;
- play is often difficult to separate from work;
- good, carefully planned and well-organized resourcing is essential to the provision of fully effective play. By providing time, space and resources teachers can extend the quality of children's talk;
- teachers need to constantly monitor children's talk as they play;
- it is helpful to chart progress and ensure play activities are coherent.

KEY POINTS

Play is central to children's learning.

Language development is enhanced through play.

Appropriate and diverse resources support progress in speaking and listening.

Young children's talk provides insight into their learning needs.

Teachers' Notes 1

BEARS: KS 1

Aims:
1. To build upon children's awareness of books about bears.
2. To develop storytelling skills; to encourage play and role play.

Objectives:
1. Telling stories.
2. Participating in imaginative play and drama.

Group size: pairs/small groups.

Timing: 35 minutes.

Organization:
1. The children or teacher should cut out the three bear cards.
2. Later, the children or teacher cut out the bear parts and use staples or split pins to put the bear together.

Resources: scissors, colours, split pins, fiction and non-fiction books about bears.

What to do:
1. Once the children have got their bear cards, they can use them in a variety of ways:
   • they can try to identify the types of bear: panda, honey and grizzly bears.
   • they can look in non-fiction books for information about each bear;
   • they can tell each other about a bear story they remember.
2. The children can make their bears and use them to act out a story about a hungry bear. Does he like honey, like Pooh; marmalade, like Paddington; or porridge, like the bears in Goldilocks? Does he like something else? What will the bears take to the teddy bears' picnic? Who else will be going to the woods today?

Cross-curricular links:
Technology: design a bed/house/waterproof coat etc. for your bear.
Drama: make up a stick-puppet play about your bear (mount the bears on card and attach to a ruler or long paint brush).
Art and Craft: make a felt bear puppet or finger puppets.
Science: let the children write their own reference books about bears.
English: make a collection of bear poems and jokes.
Maths: measure the paper bears, invent some bear sums.

Follow-up activities/extensions:
• Hold a teddy bears' picnic, encouraging parents, siblings and teddy bears from home to join in.
• Bring in some of your own and the rest of the staff's old teddy bears and have a 'Guess the name/weight/age/owner' competition.
• Make teddy bear-shaped biscuits.
• Learn some songs about bears.
• Act out *The Bear Hunt* (Michael Rosen) as a class or for an assembly.
• Create an awareness-raising assembly about the plight of bears around the world.
• Let the children act out a well-known story which includes bears.

Photocopiable Sheet 1

BEARS

ISLANDS/PIRATES: KS 2

Aims:
1. To encourage accuracy in description.
2. To encourage careful listening.
3. To sequence and then retell a story, using picture prompts.

Objectives:
1. Incorporating relevant detail in descriptions.
2. Listening carefully.
3. Sequencing pictures to tell a story.

Group size: pairs.

Timing: 15 minutes.

Organization: before the lesson, you will need to cut out the two island cards. Put A's together in one envelope and B's in another. Child A should only look at card A and child B should only look at card B. Next give each child an envelope of a set of pirate story pictures.

Resources: scissors, colours, Blu-Tack, paper, envelopes.

What to do:
1. Make sure the children sit back to back or use tall books to hide their islands from each other. A starts by asking questions about B's island. The children take it in turns to ask questions and slowly, through talking, they should be able to draw in the missing details on their own island. Tell them in advance that there are three things on the other person's island they have to find out about. When they have finished, they can compare maps.
2. Give each pair the story pictures. They should cut up the pictures, sequence them and retell the story, alternating the pictures and storytelling.

Cross-curricular links:
Geography: the children can invent an island together and 'bury' some treasure for another pair to try and find.
English: they can make up, tell or act out a story about pirates; act out the story in the pictures and devise own endings, write messages in (paper) bottles to find on the classroom 'shore' next morning.
PE: play 'pirates'.
Technology: make a treasure chest with a hinged lid.
History: find out about some famous pirates from the past, e.g. Grace O'Malley.

Follow-up activities/extensions: create treasure trails to encourage the writing and reading of instructions.

ISLANDS/PIRATES

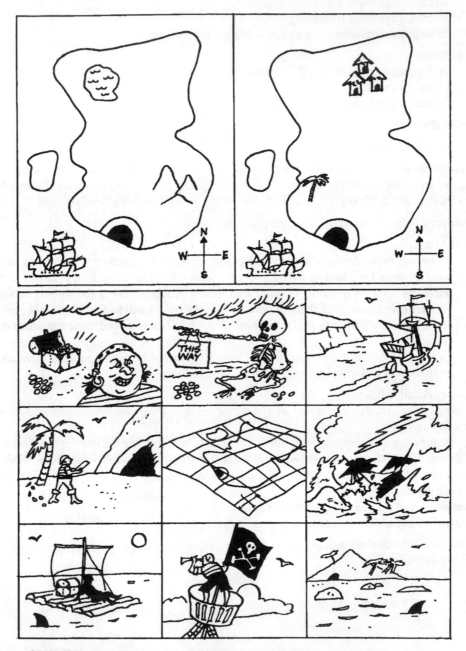

Chapter 3

Questioning, Arguing and Reasoning

Rosemary Stickland

The author is a class teacher and has responsibility for language throughout a large primary school situated in Oxfordshire. She has taught in the junior year groups in the school, Years 4, 5 and 6, and is now teaching in Reception and Year 1.

BACKGROUND

Becoming part of the National Oracy Project had a major influence on my classroom practice. It made me aware of how much talking I did and how few opportunities I created for the pupils to talk and listen to each other. Once I started trying to create those opportunities, I realized that the pupils needed to be given lots of practice in listening actively to each other, needed to be taught how to ask open questions, how to negotiate with each other and make group decisions. We experimented with different methods of grouping, getting to grips with ground rules and trying out different talk activities.

This chapter should be seen as providing starting points for developing the skills needed to reason and argue effectively. Many of the examples have been used within Early Years teaching as well as later in the school system. These skills are life-training skills and can be encouraged from a very early age.

AIMS

In this chapter, the aim is to describe the activities which I use in my classroom to develop the pupils' skills of arguing and reasoning by:

- listening to another point of view and perhaps adjusting one's own;
- disagreeing politely;

- making decisions together – negotiating;
- learning to ask open-ended questions;
- enabling pupils to learn to think critically thus enabling them to develop arguing and reasoning skills;
- enabling them to express their own opinions while actively listening to the ideas and views of others;
- enabling them to work co-operatively in a group.

STARTING OUT

Effective communication

The starting points for effective communication are good listening skills. Pupils need to be given the opportunity to experience and understand what it means to listen effectively. The benefits of this experience are an increase in confidence when talking to each other and to the class, the ability to talk easily to everyone in the class, an improvement in bonding as a group, the ability to ask open-ended questions, an extension of the range of questions asked, and the confidence to disagree politely and state one's own views. These then are the pre-requisites for good argument and reasoning skills.

Other benefits are an increased ability to move from discussion in pairs to small groups, increased ability to plan their own work in groups and take responsibility for their own learning, an improvement in making decisions in a small group, confidence in asking relevant questions of visitors to the classroom, and an ability to review their talk and to reflect on success and failures.

Getting started

In order to encourage the pupils to listen to each other, it is important that they should be able to see each other. Sitting in a circle (teacher too), should therefore be the first thing the pupils get used to doing. If necessary, arrange the furniture in the classroom in order to be able to seat all the pupils in a circle. Beg or borrow some cushions if the carpet area is not big enough.

Sitting in a circle can be fun (for all age ranges) by playing some simple clapping games, passing a pattern of claps round from pupil to pupil, or clapping out the pattern of syllables in each of their names. It is important to explain how important it is to have eye-contact with each other when we are talking and listening. Even some adults find eye-contact difficult and games help the pupils to get used to maintaining eye-contact and help also to establish relationships. Try these:

ACTIVITY BOX 1

Zoom

Look at the person on your left, say 'zoom'. That person then turns to the person sitting on his left, looks and says 'zoom', and so 'zoom' is passed round the circle. Insist on eye contact before 'zoom' can be passed on.

Tic and Toc

Following the rules for 'zoom' pass 'tic' to the person on your left and 'toc' to the person on your right and hope they both come back to you.

Throwing a face

Make a face. 'Take it off' by passing your hands over your face. Look hard at someone in the circle and 'throw' the face. The pupil should 'catch' it by making the same face and then should look at someone else to throw it to. No names should need to be spoken if good eye contact is being made.

The most important rule for talking in a circle is, *'One voice at a time.'*

The teacher will find that the pupils respond to a quiet reminder of this rule when necessary and indeed get used to reminding each other.

Getting to know and trust each other

Successful pair work depends on the pupils getting to know each other, getting to feel comfortable with each other, in short, getting to trust each other. Working regularly in a circle is an important part of building up trust, and circle games are a way of establishing relationships (see Activity Box 2).

Talking in pairs

I use the familiar formula of news-time as a way of introducing Key Stage 1 pupils to active listening and talking in pairs. Thought must be given first as to how you organize very young children into pairs.

1. You can ask them to find a friend. This can lead to the same pupils being left out; it depends on the personalities in the class.
2. Ask them to measure hands and pair off those who have roughly the same size of hands. Pupils never seem to tire of this strategy.
3. Stop any partner talk game (as described in the first section) and ask them to keep their partner.

ACTIVITY BOX 2

Magic Signpost
Ask the pupils to stand in a circle. One pupil stands in the centre with both hands held straight out to the sides and he starts to turn around slowly. He stops on command and has to name the two pupils he is pointing to.

Roundabout
One half of the class sits in a tight circle, facing outwards. The others choose someone to sit down in front of. Make sure all the pupils are facing each other before you begin. Ask them to take it in turns to tell each other something, e.g. their favourite food. Ask the outer circle to move one place round to the left until they are sitting in front of a new partner and give them a new subject to talk about.

Magic Sand
The pupils should all be sitting in a circle. Ask them to cup their hands ready to receive some magic sand you are going to pass around the circle. The sand is magic because you can't see it but you can hear it. Pour it very carefully and slowly into the pupil's hands making a suitable sound as you do so. The pupils either copy your sound or make up one of their own.

Trace a Shape
This game needs the pupils to be in pairs. Finding a partner can be bewildering at first. A useful strategy which pupils seem to enjoy is to find someone in the class who has roughly the same size hands. Once they are in pairs, ask them to sit down on the carpet facing their partner. One pupil closes his eyes while the other traces a simple shape on the palm of their partner's hand. The partner has to guess the shape and they swop roles.

Guess your partner
One half of the class sit in a line, eyes closed. The others choose a partner, sit in front of him, gently take his hand and let him feel part of their hair, face, clothing, something as a clue to their identity. At a signal, they go back to their original places while the others open their eyes and go and sit in front of the pupil they think had been their partner.

Once they are in pairs, ask them to find two chairs and to seat themselves facing each other.

The next step is to ask them to take it in turns to tell each other their news. Tell them you are going to be looking out for those who are looking at the partner, who is talking and listening well to what they are saying. Give them a few minutes and use the time to stand back and enjoy observing your class without interruptions.

Finally, ask them to come back and sit in the big circle on the carpet and once settled, ask who would like to tell their partner's news to the class.

Encourage them to keep looking round the circle rather than at you all the time. Praise any efforts and gradually all the pupils improve at remembering details.

New partners

Once the pupils are used to talking with a partner the next step is to introduce moving around to new partners. Ask them to decide who is going to be, for instance, a circle and who is going to be a triangle (or any subjects connected with the current topic). Ask the 'circles' to stand behind their chairs and look round to see who they might like to sit down and talk to next. On a given signal the 'circles' move to sit beside their new partner and begin to talk. The process is then repeated with the 'triangles' moving to a new partner. Again they should end the session by coming back to the big circle and sharing any interesting news they have heard from their partners.

CASE STUDY 1: TALKING IN PAIRS

Pupils in my reception/Year 1 class used the *talking in pairs* method to make a class decision about what theme we should have next for our play corner. They first talked in pairs sharing all their ideas. Everyone then reported back on the carpet and I made a list on the board. I then gave each pair two slips of paper on which to write their two favourite choices from the list on the board. We then came back to the carpet again and each pupil put up his choice on the board with Blu-Tack. The same choices were stuck together and excitement mounted as it became clear that 'castle' had won nine votes and would be our next theme.

MOVING ON

Learning to ask open questions is a very important part of learning to argue and reason. Opportunities to ask questions can be made part of all the talking activities so far described. A useful starting point is 'showing time' (this is when pupils have the opportunity to show something of interest they have brought to school).

Ask the pupils to put anything they want to show in the middle of the big circle. Give them a short while to look at everything and then ask if anyone wants to ask a question about anything they see on the carpet. They usually start with:

'Who brought . . . in?

and then you can encourage further questions of the proud owner:

'Where did you get it?'

is very common and is a good start. It is important to tell the pupils you want open questions which need a longer answer than just 'Yes' or 'No'. Suggest and encourage questions such as:

'Why did you bring it in?'
'What does it do?'
'Why do you like it?'

After a time the pupils become practised questioners and never tire of this particular form of showing time.

ACTIVITY BOX 3

Hot Seat

This is another enjoyable way to encourage good questions. When someone in the class tells you he has been on an outing, put him in the 'hot seat'. Seat him in a special chair (it could be yours) and announce that this person has something interesting to talk about and the class have to find out about it by asking questions. Let him choose who to ask each time and praise those questions which require a long answer. The pupils do progress from the simple:

'Where did you go?'
'What did you do?'
'What were the boring parts?'
'What were the exciting parts?'

The pupils also enjoy being asked to sit in the hot seat as a character from a favourite story. With young pupils you might ask one of them to be Father or Mother Bear or indeed Goldilocks. With older pupils you might want to introduce this technique into a humanities topic and question a blacksmith from an Anglo-Saxon village.

Once the pupils are used to talking in pairs through regular news-time active listening sessions and are becoming skilled at asking open questions, then Sheet 1, 'The Class Trip', is an easy way to introduce the process of decision-making to a Key Stage 1 (ages 5 to 7) class. Sheet 2, 'Playground Rules', takes the pupils on a stage further as the pictures encourage a lot of discussion and justification of choices.

Once the pupils get used to talking in pairs, the next stage is to bring pairs together to form small groups of four. Talking in larger groups needs different skills and a sensible starting point is the making up of ground rules. Before you start, it is worthwhile making clear the various steps you are going to take them through in order to carry out the exercise. The stages they will go through will provide a model for any future decision-making exercises.

ACTIVITY BOX 4

Decision-making

1. Provide each group with slips of blank paper – they should choose a scribe – one idea per slip of paper. (Emphasize that at this stage *every* idea should be accepted.)
2. They should make two piles of ideas, one worthy of further discussion and one for discarding.
3. Look at the pile of 'possibles' and put in order of priority by shifting around the slips.
4. Choose the three most important ideas to bring back to share with the big circle.

Once back together, each group should share their ideas by attaching the slips to the board with Blu-Tack. When everyone has had their turn, it will probably be seen that many ideas are similar. The whole group can now help to group similar ideas together and suggest headings for the categories which emerge. The resultant set of ground rules should then be made into a poster for display. You will find this way of working to be a useful model to follow in any subsequent discussion activities you wish to undertake with the class.

CASE STUDY 2: GROUND RULES MADE UP BY A YEAR 4/5 CLASS

1. Be sensible.
2. Keep discussion going — make it interesting.
3. Speak clearly.
4. Look at the person who is talking.
5. Keep on task.
6. Don't butt in.
7. Don't fidget.
8. No shouting.
9. Listen to the person who is talking.

IN FULL SWING

Showing time in the big circle helps to raise the pupils' awareness of open questions. Stories can help to introduce them to the kind of questions and statements which create a fruitful argument. If you create a situation where the pupils feel truly involved in the issues, then statements such as, 'I don't agree with that!', are made spontaneously by pupils as young as five and six years.

ACTIVITY BOX 5

Take a Story

Take a story such as *The Great Jam Sandwich by* John Vernon Lord, in which the mayor decides to hold a council meeting to try and solve the problem of the millions of wasps which are plaguing the town. Stop the story before the scene in which the council meets, and take on the role of mayor with all the pupils as the councillors. It helps create an adult-like atmosphere if you address the pupils as 'Miss' and 'Mr'. You will be inundated with amazing solutions and you will only have to ask once 'Who agrees with . . . ?' to set the scene for a polite argument with everyone addressing each other formally as long as you remain in role as chairman. Thus a polite phrase, useful in argument, can be introduced, as well as a real reason for asking the question 'Why?'

So far we have concentrated on questions for information. Now we are seeking to set up situations where the pupils need to be introduced to questions which look for the reasons for points of view. Questions such as 'Why?' and 'What are your reasons for . . . ?' and 'What do you mean by . . . ?' should be used by the teacher in the role of chairman.

Older pupils, especially when discussing something in a chosen or assigned role, will often use useful formal phrases spontaneously. These need to be picked up, praised and encouraged for them to become part of the class 'discussion vocabulary'. For younger pupils, they will more often need to be introduced by the teacher in role, although some formal phrases will arise spontaneously.

Establishing ground rules is an important part of group discussion. Once pupils have made ground rules they need practise these. A structured way to introduce them to negotiating and making decisions is the 'Statement Game'. (See *Photocopiable Sheet 4,* for an example of statements I have used with age range 9 to 11. These statements were put together by pupils after reading and discussing *The Paperbag Princess* by R. Munsch.) To organize the class into larger units, see *Photocopiable Sheet 4,* 'The Balloon Debate'.

Pupils need to be given the opportunity to reflect on their learning. The video camera is a very useful tool to aid the pupils in reflecting on the quality of their group discussion. A group in a Year 4/5 class (ages 9 to 10) taped themselves discussing what they should jettison from their balloon. The class then watched the video and picked out useful phrases some of the pupils had used which kept the debate going and avoided confrontation and confusion.

For example:

'That's interesting, would you repeat that please?'
'Who would like to go first?'
'Can I make a point please?'

Another way to organize groups is to use what is called the *Jigsaw* method (see Chapter 1). Case Study 3 is an example of this in action.

CASE STUDY 3: OUR VILLAGE

Our topic was OUR VILLAGE and the aim was to produce a comprehensive guide to it, the kind of booklet a newcomer to the area would find useful. The class by then had had a lot of experience in small group discussion and when it came to forming groups for this work chose to form mixed-sex groups because they felt from past experience that these gave a more balanced point of view.

This particular activity lent itself well to the Jigsaw method of grouping. It was organized as follows. First of all the class decided on the chapter headings using the same method described for ground rules. These were:

1. What to do in the village.
2. Local employers.
3. Schools and play-groups.
4. Shops and facilities.

The class divided themselves into groups of four. (Luckily we were a class of twenty-eight otherwise two pupils would have worked as one.) Each pupil in the group assumed one of the above numbers, taking the main responsibility within the group for writing the section relating to their number. Thus each group would in the end produce one hand-written copy of their booklet, each chapter having been written by a member of the group. This copy would then be photocopied four times so that everyone could have their own copy.

From time to time all the Ones would get together to share information and help each other write it up, similarly all the Twos, the Threes, and the Fours. This sharing and writing took up quite a lot of class time but it left me free to help where needed. Some sessions consisted of the main groups getting together in order to compare how far they had got and discuss improvements or layout or illustrations.

The information was gathered by means of local visits and 'press conferences' to which the pupils involved would invite, by letter, local people from whom they needed to get information. We went into role for these conferences, the pupils taking on the part of local reporters. An amazing variety of people came into our classroom, from the bank manager to the press officer at a big pharmaceutical research company. We heard about the security measures at our local D I Y(Do It Yourself) shop, the way new ideas are discussed at our local Community Council e.g. measures for crime prevention, what a police cell looks like, and the latest plans for the new playground in the village. It was the richest experience the pupils had that year in terms of bringing the outside world into the classroom.

At the very end, once the booklets had finally been produced, more letters were sent out to the people who had come in to help us, this time inviting them to a tea party and to view a display of all the work that had been produced. It was a very enjoyable end to the whole project.

Planning for review and reflection

Once the ground rules have been established you can introduce the pupils to the need for regular reflection sessions on how their discussions are going. This process can be introduced early on even with young pupils. A good way to start is in the big circle by asking them to tell the class about any problems they had in their group, or be positive and ask them to describe what went well. At first the problems are all to do with the pupils not getting on and you have to keep reminding them of the agreed ground rules and emphasize the positive aspects they are achieving, such as looking at each other while talking and listening, or using useful phrases such as 'You go first'. Older pupils can usually review their talk in their small groups, using the ground rules for reference, before bringing back a summary of their reflections to the whole class.

An important aspect of transforming the classroom into a discussion forum is to review what takes place and assess individual development e.g.

1.   By observing your class in action, for instance:

Key Stage 1 (ages 5 to 7): talking in pairs during a newstime session gives you time to observe and make notes;

Key Stage 2 (ages 9 to 11): the statement game frees you to observe and listen.

Both the above kinds of activity enable the teacher to focus on specific skills, e.g. argument.

2. By listening to the children reflecting together in the big circle on problems they had in their groups as well as their successes;
3. By paying particular attention to the questions pupils ask because their level of enquiry reflects the quality of their understanding and reasoning.

CASE STUDY 4: REVIEWING A DISCUSSION

Girl 1:   'Altogether, what do you think . . . how do you think our discussion went?'

Boy 1:   'I thought it went okay because we argued politely a lot . . .'

Girl 2:   'Not shouting . . .'

Girl 1:   'We did most of the things there' (pointing to the poster of class ground rules for discussion groups).

Boy 2:   'We weren't butting in.'

Boy 1:   'Keep on task . . .'

Girl 2:   'We weren't shouting like the time we had that big group altogether and we all started shouting and it was chaos.'

Girl 1:   'I think it's nice to keep to a small group'

Boy 1:   'Yeah!'

Girl 2:   'I think four is average.'

Girl 1:   'Because with four, you can discuss quietly.'

Boy 1:   'Something like two boys and two girls.'

Boy 2:   'Yeah!'

Girl 1:   'I think it's easier to discuss with boys and girls because you can get the boys' ideas and the girls' ideas.'

(This group had just finished discussing gender statements in a statement game.)

Girl 1:   'So you think our discussion got on well?'

General voice: 'Yeah!'

Boy 1:   'Mainly because we never stopped talking.'

KEY POINTS

Questioning skills need to be practised.

Use a variety of strategies and groupings.

Encourage pupils to ask each other for clarification.

Share the spirit of enquiry.

Time needs to be given for reflection.

Involve all the pupils in discussions and in generating questions.

Open-ended questions encourage talk and thought.

Never denigrate a pupil's question.

Sit back and let the pupils take control.

> **Teachers' Notes 1**

SCHOOL TRIP

Aim: to introduce the skills of making decisions together, justifying opinions, negotiation.

Objectives:
1.   Understanding the process of negotiation.
2.   Knowing how to present an argument.

Group size: pairs.

Organization: teacher decides which children will work together. Children can work at their tables or in other areas of the classroom. Introduction and review are whole-class activities.

Timing: 10 minutes in pairs; 15 to 20 minutes whole class.

Resources: one sheet of paper per pair; a pair of scissors per pair; a sheet of paper marked YES in one half and NO in the other.

What to do:
1.   Ask the children in their pairs to take turns to cut up the picture along the black lines.
2.   Ask them to decide together which pictures should go in the YES box and which in the NO box.
3.   They should *both* agree which pictures should go in which box. Ask them to talk about their reasons for deciding on the boxes.
4.   If they *cannot* decide, ask them to leave that picture to one side.
5.   Finally, they should then look at the YES box and decide on three pictures to bring back to the big circle.

Big circle: There are various ways of sharing their results:
1.   Each pair could Blu-Tack their three pictures onto the board. You then group the pictures in order to see what the class as a whole thought were the three most important items to take on a school trip.
2.   Each pair could choose the most important item, Blu-Tack the picture on the board and explain to the whole group their reasons for choosing it.
3.   You ask the pairs to talk about the items they could not agree upon.

Review: allow time for the children to reflect on any problems they encountered as well as what they enjoyed most about the exercise.

Cross-curricular links: geography.

Follow-up activities/extensions: the results could be made into a graph.

Ask the pairs to meet up as fours and bring back to the big circle what the group thought were the three most important items.

Older children could do without pictures and be asked to write down results of the group brainstorm – then prioritize: e.g. items for a school trip for four days; items you would need for survival on a desert island; items you would most want to have in your hand baggage on discovering you had lost your luggage at the airport at the beginning of a foreign holiday.

Photocopiable Sheet 1

SCHOOL TRIP

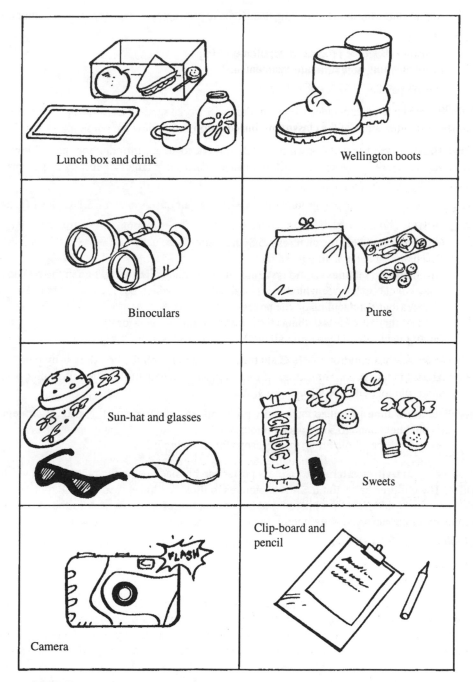

Lunch box and drink

Wellington boots

Binoculars

Purse

Sun-hat and glasses

Sweets

Camera

Clip-board and pencil

Teachers' Notes 2

PLAYGROUND RULES

Aim: to introduce the skills of making decisions, justifying opinions, negotiation, empathy.

Objectives:
1. Learning about the process of decision-making.
2. Understanding how rules are formulated.
3. Appreciating other people's opinions.

Group size: pairs.

Timing: 10 minutes in pairs; 15 to 20 minutes whole class.

Organization: teacher decides which children work together. Introduction and review are whole-class activities, otherwise children can work at their tables or in other appropriate areas of the classroom.

Resources: per pair: one playground picture sheet; a pair of scissors; YES/NO sheet (p. 54).

What to do
1. Children should cut the pictures along the black lines.
2. Discuss what each picture is 'saying'.
3. Decide which pictures should go in the YES box and which should go in the NO box.
4. They should both agree which pictures should go in which box. Ask them to talk about their reasons for deciding on the boxes.
5. If they cannot decide, ask them to leave that picture to one side.
6. Finally they should then bring all the YES pictures back to the big circle.

Big circle: Ask the children to Blu-Tack their YES pictures on the board, pair by pair. This should result in four groups of pictures. From each picture, help the children formulate a useful ground rule for behaviour in the playground.

Review: allow time for reflection on any problems encountered and thinking of strategies which would help pairs to solve disagreements.

Cross-curricular links: RE, personal and social education

Follow-up activities/extensions: a class poster can be made using the pictures and written rules. The children can paint their own pictures to illustrate the agreed rules. Experience of this activity would help the children make up ground rules for behaviour in the classroom. Older children can bypass the picture stage and start from prioritizing written ideas, and progress to a class poster.

PLAYGROUND RULES

THE BALLOON DEBATE: CHILDREN'S RIGHTS

Aim: to learn how to prioritize and negotiate, taking other people's opinions into account.

Objectives:
1. Making opinions explicit.
2. Listening to others' points of view, evaluating information in order to come to a decision.

Group size: children should work in groups of six.

Timing: 30 minutes (can be extended).

Organization: teacher decides on which children will work together. Teacher to provide the material for discussion.

Resources: cut up the statements and give out to each group.

What to do: ask the children to imagine they are in a balloon, enjoying a lovely, peaceful ride, when, suddenly they realize the balloon is losing height. In order to save a crash landing, they must throw out one of the boxes in the basket. There are six boxes, each labelled with a 'right'. Which box should go first?

In their groups, each child takes on the task of defending a box and, in turn, they should try to give reasons why it is important enough NOT to be thrown out. The group then has the hard task of deciding which box should be thrown out.

In the big circle, each group should report back on which box they decided to throw out and why.

Cross-curricular links: can be linked to most subject areas. Very useful for RE and personal social education (PSE).

Follow-up activities/extensions:
1. The children could empathize with any group in society and make up a set of their rights for a similar balloon debate.
2. More than one box could be thrown out OR try to decide on the ONE box to be kept in.

THE BALLOON DEBATE: CHILDREN'S RIGHTS

1.	The right to a bedroom of your own.

2.	The right to love and affection.

3.	The right to pocket money.

4.	The right to clean air.

5.	The right to be educated.

6.	The right to play.

Teachers' Notes 4

THE STATEMENT GAME

Aim: for children to experience negotiating a concensus and understand the need for negotiation.

Objectives:
1.   To listen to others' opinions.
2.   To justify own opinions.
3.   To clarify what has been said.
4.   To understand how negotiation takes place.

Group size: two to four children.

Timing: 30 minutes (this can be extended as appropriate).

Organization: teacher decides which children will work together. Teacher provides the materials. Children can work at their own tables or in appropriate areas of the classroom.

Resources: board or large sheet of paper, halved, with AGREE in one half and DISAGREE in the other half.

What to do:
Each pair should have a statement board and the ten statements cut up.
1.   The children start in pairs, read through the statements, and decide which box to place each statement in. They must BOTH agree on a box before a statement is placed in it. Encourage questioning and justification of a point of view. The statements are not meant to be quickly tossed in without a lot of reasoned discussion.
2.   The pairs then meet up and in fours compare what they have done. There may be statements which could not be decided on and these are good ones to start the discussion with, looking to see if a decision can be reached.
3.   In the big circle it is often most interesting to have each group report back on the statement which caused most controversy. Some can then be flung open to general discussion.

Cross-curricular links: any subject area, also RE and personal and social education.

Follow-up activities/extensions:
1.   Issue books on the subject can be read and discussed, e.g. *Piggy* book by Anthony Browne, *The Paperbag Princess* by Robert Munsch.
2.   Children can be asked to make up their own statements on another theme; it could be taken from a story, or from a history topic.

Photocopiable Sheet 4

THE STATEMENT GAME

Girls run faster than boys.

Boys are better at sewing than girls.

Girls are bossier than boys.

Boys are quieter than girls.

Girls have better handwriting than boys.

Girls are better at football.

Boys shouldn't learn cooking at school.

Boys are better at making things than girls.

Boys take up all the room in the playground.

Girls are tidier than boys.

Chapter 4

SACLA: A Systematic and Co-operative Learning Approach to Group Work in the Classroom

Candace Savory

The author has recently completed her doctorate: the focus of her research was the educational and social impact of a systematic approach to co-operative learning in the primary classroom. She has worked extensively with primary teachers and pupils to enhance awareness of team and group work techniques, building upon an approach to team work which was developed for use in business and industry.

BACKGROUND

In her search for relevant methods of group work training, she recognized the substantial work carried out in the area of organizational management. She became interested in the Coverdale Organization whose structured approach to group work, based on people learning from their own experience, appeared to have great potential in being adapted for children. Systematic And Co-operative Learning Approach (SACLA as it became known) is the group work approach she developed through adaptation of the Coverdale method for co-operative learning. Over seventy teachers, both primary and secondary, have so far been trained to use it, with encouraging results.

AIMS

The general aims of this chapter are:

1. to highlight the main principles and practices involved;
2. to show how the approach can be implemented.

In order for children to learn the skills required to co-operate with each other, and operate a common method of action, research evidence indicates that they need to be taught those skills explicitly.

The aims of SACLA are:

- To help children learn the skills needed to work with others – both their co-operative skills and their planning, problem-solving and self-organizing abilities.
- To provide children with a common method/language for working together.
- To satisfy the NC Programmes of Study for English (Speaking and Listening).
- To encourage an appreciation amongst pupils of the processes of group work and effective learning.
- To enable teachers to manage groups more effectively and to assess group work.

It involves groups of five or six children, by means of carefully set tasks, in learning through structured cycles of Preparation, Action and Review within a systematic framework of getting things done. This framework is known by the children as a Systematic Approach. It consists of a series of stages, through which the children are trained to consider and agree:

1. Why they are doing a particular activity: what and who it is for?
2. What they want to end up with.
3. The standards by which they can measure their achievement.
4. Ideas and relevant information.
5. What has to be done (WHTBD).
6. Who is going to do what – how and when.
7. Followed by Action when they do the task, after which they:
8. Review successes and difficulties experienced, identifying the causes in order to make plans to improve in the future.

The tasks are short and fairly 'natural', so that more attention can be devoted by the children to the way they are working, rather than becoming absorbed by task completion alone.

Each child has the opportunity of 'observing' her group do a task in order to develop her observation skills, raise her awareness of where the group is 'at' and to give practice in feeding back factual observations during the review.

Approximately twelve training sessions are carried out in the initial phase of SACLA training. Ideally these take place intensively over a period of two to four weeks in the classroom. During approximately the first six training sessions, emphasis is on coming to grips with the steps of Systematic Approach and developing self-organizing skills. The latter sessions focus increasingly on themes such as listening and support, while continuing to give practice in Systematic Approach. Once the initial SACLA training phase is completed, there is a transition from training-type tasks to tasks that are directly related to the curriculum.

STARTING OUT

Implementing the programme

The following task is the first task of the training programme, the same instruction being given to each group in the class:

TASK INSTRUCTION

'Carry out a survey of cars in the school car park.'

(Time allowed: 45 minutes)

The design of the 'open' task is driven by the following learning purposes:

- chiefly, to raise awareness of the need for PURPOSE;
- to provide experience of working together on a SINGLE task;
- to raise awareness of the need for a METHOD of working together.

The task is open in the sense that Purpose is needed to decide what sort of information to collect. The options can only be 'closed down' by deciding on Purpose.

The teacher's role

Divide the class into groups. Give each group the task and the time limit which needs to be adhered to. Observe the groups while on task. It is better to choose one or two groups to observe rather than hop from one group to the other. This enables one to spend adequate time with each, to make accurate, albeit fewer observations.

On being given the first task, pupils tend to rush into action, and may not produce a task result. A possible outcome of the task is that groups do define a purpose. For example, one group of 9-year-olds planned to show which cars belonged to which teachers, while the other groups simply collected a catalogue of facts from car colour to registration number and hence were confused about what to do with the information. Most commonly, the question of 'Why?' is not discussed, and it is not until the review stage that the lesson about the need to ask 'Why' is learned from their own experience. You may need to probe the group during review as to the causes of their confusion in order to draw out the lesson about the need for a clear purpose. At least 25 minutes should be allowed for the group reviews at the end of a task. The review model is basically as follows (get the children to divide their chart into three areas):

a) Successes (e.g. We all had something to do)	*Cause?* (e.g. We divided the jobs up equally)	
b) Difficulties (e.g. We were confused)	*Cause?* (e.g. Didn't discuss Purpose)	*c) Plan to improve* (e.g. Decide WHY we're doing it)

Brief the class on the review model and the sort of review questions to consider, for example: 'Have we achieved what we set out to do?' (task consideration), 'What did people do or say that helped?' (process considerations).

Encourage the taking forward of lessons from one task to the next, by reminding groups to refer to their improvement plans at the start of the next task. Also useful are personal review notebooks in which the children can record individual thoughts on a regular basis. By so doing, they become involved in charting their own progress in group work. After the group reviews, get the class together and ask each group to report on their task results and the results of their reviews, including their plans for improvement next time, e.g. the need to discuss Purpose.

After this first task, you can then introduce Systematic Approach, building as much as possible on what comes out of the children's own experience of their first task and review. It is given as a framework or a common language to help them work together better (see ***Photocopiable Sheets 1 and 2).***

MOVING ON

The second task

The following task is the second task of the training programme and useful at motivating the children into action:

TASK INSTRUCTION

'Draw a diagram of the classroom with movable pieces of card to represent the furniture, to help the teacher look at different arrangements of the room.'

(Time allowed: 45 minutes)

The design of the above 'closed' task is driven by the following learning purposes:

- to raise awareness of information (WHTBD), and planning stages;
- to check purpose and relate activity to it.

The task is closed in the sense that purpose is given and the end result is clear, so careful planning is needed. There are clearly two action stages: the children need to get information (by going into action at the information step of Systematic Approach) and then carry out the task once they have planned it (action proper).

The importance of observation and review

The practice of observation by children is started in Task 2. Brief one member of each group to act as observer – this role is rotated each task. Brief observers to note when someone does or says something which really helps the group. You may want to vary the brief from task to task, depending on what you want them to observe, for example, 'How much they were co-operating?' – see *Photocopiable Sheet 3* for an Observation Brief on Co-operation.

While you yourself observe the groups on task, look particularly at the extent to which groups are using the Systematic Approach framework, if at all:

1.　Observe for definite planning, as opposed to improvisation.

2.　Observe for relationship between plans made and purpose of task.

3.　Draw out any valuable lessons on the review, particularly in respect of information, WHTBD and planning.

It is important that groups chart the stages of Systematic Approach as early as possible. It becomes an important focus for both sharing and eliciting information. For example, at the ideas/information stage, pupils who make their own notes in a group often waste time in generating contradictory ideas, whereas if the ideas are charted on a central chart, the pupils often build on each other's ideas to reach more quickly an acceptable picture of an end result.

The 'open' and 'closed' theme continues for several tasks with the children developing skills in using the different stages of Systematic Approach. Timing is always an important feature of these early SACLA sessions. Children are often unused to working to a deadline and should be encouraged to review and reflect upon their own individual management of the time allowed. Reviews are in fact an essential part of SACLA group work. Time is given at the end of each task to draw out 'process' lessons, in order to plan improvements in this area the next time the group work together. The practice of review and observation helps develop the children's assessment skills, enabling them to become more aware of both their own progress and that of the group.

IN FULL SWING

The following case studies illustrate SACLA being used by two groups who were familiar with the approach.

CASE STUDY 1: REFINING GROUP WORK SKILLS

The following task was given to a group of 11-year-olds around session eight of the programme. It is inadvisable to give it before the children have developed adequate skill in using Systematic Approach as a framework of communication.

TASK INSTRUCTION

'Design and test a new game.'
(Time allowed: 45 minutes)

The teacher's design of the above 'open' task was driven by the following learning purposes:

* practice in listening and building on other's ideas;
* practice in aims – purpose, visualizing end-result, setting standards.

Before the above task was given, the teacher had a class session on listening, discussing what stages are involved in active listening, in order to help the children analyse the listening process. The teacher then briefed the children to draw up a list of ideas on what makes a good listener and a good speaker – see ***Photocopiable Sheet 4*** for the brief. The teacher discussed and charted the children's responses.

Next, the teacher briefed groups to devise a listening plan in order to improve listening in the next task and to review how they got on with it at the end. The teacher briefed the observers specifically to look for instances of active listening during this particular task. The teacher herself observed groups to see whether their listening plans were being used, and also for their use of Systematic Approach, particularly the aims of the task.

Having devised a listening plan (to go round the group, charting and discussing each person's idea in turn), the group of 11-year-olds starting on the task of designing a game. A long list of ideas was charted and the group then began choosing which to go for, listening and responding well to one another.

Because the children were struggling somewhat at the planning stage, due to their vision of end-result lacking detail, the teacher suggested they discussed questions such as, 'What exactly do we want to end up with?', 'Can we draw a rough sketch to show it?'. This helped the group visualize the end-result in more detail, which consequently helped them plan more effectively.

The group set a series of measurable standards, such as, the game had to be original and suitable for primary school children and that everyone should feel that they had had their ideas listened to. In 45 minutes, the group had produced and tested an original board game to help children to spell. They carried out a group review, with the help of the observer, identifying their successes largely by checking off all the standards they had agreed to meet. This is a summary of the review presented to the class:

Successes	*Cause*	
Met all our standards.	Set them at the start, so we knew what to aim for.	
Planning went well in the end.	Went back and drew a clearer picture of the end-result, so we could plan who does what.	
Listened well.	Followed our listening plan.	

Difficulties	*Cause*	*Plan to improve*
Bit rushed making game.	Too much time wasted trying to plan it out.	Sketch out a better picture of end-result.

CASE STUDY 2:
A CURRICULUM TASK

The next training task instruction was given to a group of 10-year-olds who had been fully trained in SACLA. Their class topic was electricity, and group work was being used by the teacher to do experiments.

TASK INSTRUCTION

'Devise a way of demonstrating to younger pupils how an electricity circuit works.'

(Time allowed: 1 hour)

The children worked through the following stages:

1. The group charted the purpose of the task and began discussing what they could do.
    'Where would you have the switches?'
    Here the children were ASKING, ANSWERING, EXPLAINING.

2. They reflected on each other's ideas.
    'If we use your idea, we will have to set the circuit up inside a box.'
    'I think it might work . . .'
    Here the children were MAKING CHOICES, DECIDING.

3. They then drew a sketch of the desired end-result (a doll's house with lights) and discussed what would go where, and so on.
    'That would have to link up to the battery . . .'
    'If we connected this . . .'
    Here the children were PREDICTING, RECORDING, TALKING AND COMMUNICATING.

4. They set standards to aim for:
   'Remember, we've got to be able to explain how it works to the little . . .'
   They discussed: 'What jobs have to be done?', 'Who wants to do what?'
   Here the children were COLLABORATING, ORGANIZING AND TAK-ING RESPONSIBILITY.

5. When the action phase began, the group experimented with the apparatus.
   Here the children were EXPLORING, INVESTIGATING, OBSERVING AND INTERPRETING.

6. Having finished the task, the group held a review of the successes and diffi-culties:
   'What was the cause of that problem, again? Oh yeh, we didn't . . .'
   Here the children were RECALLING AND REFLECTING.

Finally, the group drew up a list of plans for improvement, both in the way that they worked together and in the terms of improvements they could make to their design and demonstration.

As we can see from these two case studies, children can move from specific review discussions to consider improvements in task processes and commu-nication skills. Pupils can be encouraged to consider these skills in more general contexts, e.g. *Photocopiable Sheet 4*, which asks pupils to decide what makes effective speakers and listeners.

KEY POINTS

Skills of group work need to be learned.

Approach a task together.

Clarify the purpose of the task.

Learn from listening to each other.

Always work out a method first.

SYSTEMATIC APPROACH FOR 5- TO 7-YEAR-OLDS

Aim: to work co-operatively and methodically as a group, using a common method and language (a Systematic Approach).

Objectives:
1. Improving speaking and listening skills.
2. Improving self-organizing skills.
3. Improving task skills, e.g. writing.

Group size: three to five pupils.

Timing: 25 to 30 minutes. Training tasks are shorter for the younger age group.

Organization: Organize children into small groups. Decide the tasks, time limit and prepare materials. Encourage them to use Systematic Approach.

Resources: clear task instruction, Photocopiable Sheet 1 for each child or a large wall poster of the steps. Materials for the task. Clock to show time allowed for task (training tasks are shorter for this age group, usually 25 minutes instead of 45).

What to do: hand out Photocopiable Sheet 1 or make a poster showing the steps to do a task together. Explain that the children can refer to the steps at any time during the task. After the task, gather the groups together and review what helped things go well.

Explain each stage of Systematic Approach, using examples to build on their own experience. For example, Step 1: WHY are we doing the task? If you know *why* you are doing something, it helps you know *what* to do. If you know why your family is going out, it helps you know where to go, e.g.

To buy a present you go to town.

To play football you go to the park.

Cross-curricular links: depends on task given.

Follow-up activities/extensions: individual tasks can be used to give individual practice in using Systematic Approach.

Photocopiable Sheet 1

A SYSTEMATIC APPROACH

SYSTEMATIC APPROACH FOR 8- TO 13-YEAR-OLDS

Aim: to work co-operatively and methodically as a group, using a common method and language (Systematic Approach).

Objectives:
1. Improving speaking and listening skills.
2. Improving problem-solving and self-organizing skills.
3. Improving task skills, e.g. writing.

Group size: four to seven pupils.

Timing: 1 hour.

Organization: at the end of Stage 2 of training programme, or as early as possible, even though at first they may only use some of the steps. Organize children into small groups to do tasks. Decide the task, time limit and prepare materials.

Resources: materials for the task, clear task instructions and a chart board for each group or chart paper on wall space, to provide a clear focus for the group's brainstorm.

What to do: explain each stage of Systematic Approach, using examples to build on their own experience. For example, Step 2: Imagine the end-result. If you imagine what result you would like before you begin, it will give you some idea of how to start. If you picture what kind of present to buy for your friend's birthday before you go shopping, it helps you decide which shop to visit. Imagining the sort of result you would like before you begin a task gives you something to aim for.

Cross-curricular links: depends on task.

Follow-up activities/extensions: individual tasks can be given, to provide use of Systematic Approach.

THE ORGANIZED WAY TO DO A TASK

Tell me please how to do a task in an organised way

Just follow the steps. Easy!

Step 1: Ask yourself the reason for doing the task.

WHY am I doing the task?

Step 2: Draw or write down your ideas about what you would like to have at the end of the task.

I imagine the result to be like this...

Step 3: Write down a special list of things you want to aim for in the task, so that you try to achieve good standards of work.

I am going to set myself some standards to aim for.. like.. neatness... and following all the steps...

Step 4: Write down a list of things you *need* for the task.

I need... ink... paper... ideas... help.

Step 5: Write down what *jobs* have to be done in order to do the task properly.

W.H.T.B.D.

Step 6: Write down a list of *who* is going to do these jobs.

Step 7: THEN GO FOR IT EVERYONE.

Step 8: Review.

Look back on the task to see what went well and what needs improvement.

BRIEF FOR CHILDREN ON 'OBSERVING CO-OPERATION'

Aims:
1. To give practice in specific, factual observation.
2. To increase awareness of group processes.
3. To improve co-operative behaviour.

Objectives:
1. Improving pupils' observation and listening skills.
2. Improving pupils' self-assessment skills.

Group size: four to seven pupils.

Timing: 30 to 40 minutes or whatever is appropriate for task.

Organization: Select pupils and choose a group observer.

Resources: clearly explained observation brief for observers. Task for groups.

What to do:
1. Provide group observers with 'Observing co-operation brief', asking them to note instances of co-operative behaviour by putting a tick in the appropriate column. Ask them to try and note what was said or done, briefly, in order to provide the group with specific examples.
2. Observe groups yourself for instances of co-operative behaviour. After the task ask each of the observers to report back observations in their group's review. Hold class session afterwards to draw together lessons learned from each review.

Cross-curricular links: observation brief can apply to any curriculum task.

Follow-up activities/extensions: ask one group to observe another group, using the observing co-operation brief; each member of one group observes and feeds back about a specific person in the other group.

Photocopiable Sheet 3

'OBSERVING CO-OPERATION'

Put a tick in the column every time you observe co-operative behaviour – that means every time you observe someone:

1.   make a suggestion or give an idea
2.   reply to a suggestion of an idea
3.   ask a question so that things can move on
4.   act on someone else's suggestion, instead of just sitting there.

Try to write down what was said or done by whom.

Make a suggestion/idea	Reply to a suggestion/idea	Ask a question	Act on someone's suggestion/idea

---
Teachers' Notes 4

BRIEF FOR CHILDREN ON WHAT MAKES A GOOD LISTENER AND SPEAKER

Aims:

1. To increase awareness of what skills a good listener and speaker has.
2. To increase pupil's listening and speaking skills in the group.

Objective: improving pupil's listening and speaking skills through practice.

Group size: younger children: groups of three to five, older children: groups of four to seven.

Timing: 30–45 minutes.

Organization: address the whole class and ask pupils to carry out the exercise individually. You then collect responses to produce a central chart for the class.

Resources: Photocopiable Sheet 4.

What to do: brief the class or groups clearly. Either chart children's responses yourself in class setting, or ask groups to present their collective responses on a chart to the rest of the class.

Cross-curricular links: applies to any curriculum task.

Follow-up activities/extensions: get the children to practise speaking and listening skills through a variety of group activities or games, for example, taking it in turns to tell and build on a story, by listening carefully to what was said before.

WHAT MAKES A GOOD LISTENER AND SPEAKER?

A good listener . . .	A good speaker . . .

Chapter 5

Forging Links Between Talk and Writing

Margaret Armitage

The author of this chapter is a headteacher of a village primary school, and has extensive and varied experience teaching infants and juniors. Her emphasis has always been to encourage the children to talk about their work and she provided a variety of situations for this to develop. Her professional development was further extended through courses which provided discussion forums and frameworks for this approach. She has written widely on education.

BACKGROUND

About ten years ago, while teaching 5- and 6-year-olds, I became involved with local teachers who wanted to look more closely at children's developing writing. We wrote and talked much about writing, and began to observe children's responses to writing in the classroom.

Donald Graves' (1983) approach, which places talk at the centre of the writing process, was influential at this stage. His work showed that thinking and talking skills which even young children could develop when writing was purposeful, relevant and drew on their personal experiences.

A literature course, run by Aidan Chambers, encouraged the keeping of a personal reading journal to reflect upon the impact of the books read. It was this type of writing, a personal dialogue, which made us realize that writing can create new ideas, unlock feelings, make connections and form new perspectives. But it also required the sharing of these experiences through talk to clarify how this process worked. I began to ask how far the activities in the classroom encouraged this dynamic view of writing and talking.

The task for all teachers working with young children is to keep asking the question 'Why write?' Writing should be part of everyday reality for children. It should inform, make us think, feel and relate. It should confirm what is known and it should extend and challenge. An integral part of the process of writing is talking, sorting ideas. Although discrete processes in themselves, nevertheless writing and talk parallel and support each other. Talk can shape the writing. It is the connection between the two that this chapter is aiming to illustrate.

AIMS

There are a number of aims this chapter will address, and each applies equally to all age ranges. Younger children can be encouraged to develop their own notation systems and can be helped by adults working as scribes:

*   to encourage an awareness that there is a difference between talking and writing but that they are of equal value;
*   to develop an awareness that writing is purposeful and can make things happen;
*   to illustrate how classroom opportunities can help children use talk as a means of developing their writing;
*   to outline some of the implications for the teacher for planning and organization.
*   to consider how this approach can be shared by others in the school.

STARTING OUT

Planning links between talk and writing

When planning for opportunities in which talk and writing can support each other, we need to take account of the different genres in writing available to the writer, as well as the different registers available to the speaker. The pupils need to develop their awareness of the influence of audience and purpose, and the way these influence style. We may find the following points helpful:

*   being specific about what skills we want the children to develop in writing: note-taking? different styles? different audiences? Discussion can help clarify the differences;
*   being clear about the skills in talking we want the pupils to develop: negotiation? questioning techniques? debating? Each skill should also be discussed in relation to the writing process;

- being aware that some activities will need to be allocated specific time slots, trying to be flexible to allow for unexpected developments;
- trying to encourage the pupils of whatever age to take a role in classroom planning so that the teaching and learning are rooted in activities owned in partnership with the teacher.

One way of helping pupils to see the interdependence of talk and writing is to ask them certain questions in the early stages of their own planning. The following suggestions can be adapted to suit any age and ability of pupil:

- How can you record what you have just discussed so you won't forget?
- What questions do you need to ask?
- Where can you put the answers to your questions?
- How can you show others what you have just talked about?
- How will you show your work to others?

Noting responses such as these, which is a means to organizing ideas and thoughts, is emphasized in the National Curriculum for English. However, younger pupils need a realistic context in which this can be developed. The following examples reveal how these contexts can be provided:

a) Planning a visit

CASE STUDY 1: A DAY VISIT

A class of 27 Year 4 to 5 (ages 9 to 10) children were involved in comparing the physical geography of the home area with a contrasting locality. A great deal of work had been done both in the school grounds and surrounding area, collecting information about the local insects and plants. A visit to the White Horse Hill was planned by the pupils to discover if the chalk uplands revealed different types of habitat and species. The aim was for them to take on the responsibility and, therefore, the ownership of the event.

In pairs, the children talked about and listed all the work they thought would need to be done to prepare for the day visit. These ideas were brought together in a whole-class discussion and a common 'agenda for action' was drawn up. Pairs of children then volunteered to take responsibility for one aspect from the list. What they organized would happen and what they forgot would have real consequences. Returning from the day visit, one of the children (who was acting as navigator) became engrossed in a conversation with his friends. He forgot to tell me which way to go and a vital turning was missed. Out came the maps to find a route home, providing opportunity for discussion, negotiation, direction-giving.

There was a valid purpose in all of these activities for drafting and for good presentation. All required discussion either in small groups or as a class. The pupils realized that they had to take genuine responsibility.

Photocopiable Sheet 1: 'Getting Ideas' might be useful in encouraging pupils to think around a project they are involved in.

b) Role play
Role-play can enhance pupils' understanding of the issues they are meeting in their work. It can also create rich opportunities for writing and for 'communicating information, opinions and feelings fluently' (National Curriculum for English).

CASE STUDY 2: ENVIRONMENTAL AWARENESS

In this example a challenge was presented to the same class of 9- to 10-year-olds, which dealt with some environmental work they had been involved in. They had to take on roles both for and against the cause.

PRESERVE WHITE HORSE HILL!

You live near Uffington Village.

You have heard that a property development company wants to:

1.   build a car park next the White Horse with a toilet block;
2.   make a children's playground in the middle of Uffington Castle;
3.   build an ice-cream shop in the car park where we parked the mini-bus.

You have formed an action group to stop the development.

Make up a name for your group.

Now plan an appeal to the County Council saying why they must stop the development.

You will need to:

1.   work out what to say
2.   work out who will say it
3.   make posters, charts, maps, plans, etc. to create a good impression, that you are worth listening to
4.   prepare your presentation for Wednesday, 30 June at 1.30 p.m.

The Chairperson will say whether you have changed the County Council's mind.

The children took roles and acted out the debate.
This case study raises some important points.

> – The pupils were free to choose with whom they worked.
> – Group size was restricted to a maximum of four, preferably three. This was to ensure that every child in a group had to play a full and active part.
> – A time limit was given by which the groups had to be ready so that the children could plan out just how much they would have to achieve each session.
> – Overall, they had four hours available spread over two days.
> – A girl was chosen to act as 'Chairperson'. Her job would be to listen to the evidence and decide on a course of action for the 'Council'.

This activity posed several challenges for the children:

- the need to work co-operatively;

- all group members to be involved;

- working to a time limit;

- choice of effective style of talk/writing and suitability for the occasion;

- adopting skills in reasoning, putting forward a particular opinion and persuasive argument;

- skills of presentation in talk/writing;

- willingness to enter into debate, listen to reasoned argument and defend one's case.

The pupils sorted their ideas and presentations, making rough notes. The children approached the task by:

- listing important points they wished to put in their speech;

- numbering the points to show in which order they would be presented;

- ticking off the points once they were included in the speech.

The challenge encouraged both persuasive writing and speaking.

Photocopiable Sheet 3: 'Planning a Report' could be used to help groups prepare their ideas for a discussion or reporting back session with the class. A framework for producing a written outcome can be found in *Photocopiable Sheet 4:* 'Investigating An Insect'.

MOVING ON

Working in a variety of contexts

There should be plenty of opportunities for children to work in a variety of situations. What experiences are available in the classroom for:

- friendship/mixed ability/same ability groups?
- individual work?
- working in an undisturbed space for a considerable period of time?
- working in groups organized by the teacher/by the children?
- working as a whole class?

a) Groupings

Mixed ability pairs can work well. One pupil can act as scribe while the other pupil offers ideas and suggestions. Mixed age groups have their place too. This is where pupils with special needs can build up their confidence.

CASE STUDY 3: MIXED AGE GROUPS

One 8-year-old boy had difficulties in many areas of the curriculum. One afternoon he spent an hour in the Reception Class helping children where he could. He took charge of a group of 5-year-olds trying to plan out how to make a lighthouse. He invited all the children in the group to put forward ideas, he jotted suggestions down and then helped them draw up an agreed design. Rarely did he take such a leading role in his own class, nor was his sense of responsibility always so evident.

Other points to be considered when organizing group work:

- When pupils are working in groups, it is still important for them to share what they have done with the rest of the class. Class discussions/reporting sessions have the value of creating a sense of wholeness and unity.
- The management of class discussions needs ground rules understood by all; setting 'rules for good discussions' is a task which can be done by the pupils; the more they own them, the more likely they are to adhere to them.
- It is important to maintain a balance between the various types of grouping so that pupils can experience the different skills required in each setting.

b) Time management

Time management is perhaps the most difficult. There has to be sufficient time for the talk *and* the writing to develop, for mistakes to be found and new plans to be set. If there is a strict time limit and only certain times in the day when writing can be done, then the pressure can stifle creativity and the outcomes may be insubstantial. However, on occasions, a finishing time needs to be made clear to the pupils. Such a framework can energise the children into action and keep their minds focused on the job.

Realistic time schedules can be worked out successfully with children. By asking the question 'how much time do you think you still need?' the pupils will (after plenty of practice in this) be able to give you a very good indication of how to plan future sessions. Flexibility of timing plus clear aims and precise objectives are the key notes to good organization.

IN FULL SWING

Review and reflection

Review and reflection should take place at various stages in the process as well as at the end of the work. This particular type of talk is essential to progression and development. Evaluation may happen with individuals, small groups or whole class. Whatever the context it needs to be planned for.

Generally the questions we can try out to encourage reflection remain the same whether we are talking with one pupil or thirty.

- Tell me what you have just been working on.

- What has gone well?

- What problems have you had to deal with?

- How have you tried to overcome them?

- What will you do next?

- What have you learned particularly this session?

These questions can be applied to either the process of working or to the actual piece of work produced by the pupil or the group.

As pupils work through these questions, sometimes through discussion as a class, sometimes written as a group, the process of learning becomes evident, thinking is clarified and connections made between past, current and future learning.

Photocopiable Sheet 2: 'Looking Back/Looking Forward' can be used to highlight the importance of talk in the writing process and help children look critically at their work.

Time pressures often create situations in which it is extremely difficult to find either the time or the energy for our own reflection. This does not just mean what the outcomes were or how things went in the classroom, although one needs to consider these. What is important is a deeper kind of reflection which brings us back to the nature of learning, to the involvement and the motivation of pupils and to our role in the process of encouraging active learning.

Writing and talking are interdependent yet they are each unique ways of communicating. They have different functions, processes and outcomes but they still support and inform each other. Our classroom practice should not only highlight the differences but it should also actively encourage pupils to use one as a means of enhancing the other.

Writing and talking need realistic contexts in which pupils can acquire and practise a variety of skills and extend their understanding of communication through the spoken and the written word. Once imagination and motivation are engaged and they see a purpose for their work, then we may be surprised by their creativity, their ability to communicate effectively through talk and writing, and their acquisition of a sense of the power through both the spoken and the written word.

Photocopiable Sheet 4: 'Investigating an Insect' can be used to help children explore topics/items/issues. It provides a framework and a real outcome which they can refer to in the future.

Questions about ants asked by one group included the following:

• Are ants vertebrates?
• How many legs do ants have? How do they move?
• How many parts?
• Are ants warm blooded?
• Do ants have eyes?
• What sort of food do they eat?
• How do they catch their prey?
• Do they store food in the winter?

The approaches in this chapter can be used with pupils of different ages. The example of the older child helping reception children to discuss and formulate plans reflects how staff can collaborate and develop talking and writing skills throughout the school.

KEY POINTS

Writing tasks linked to and through discussion.

Real audiences and appropriate genres.

Interest and involvement.

Time to rehearse writing through talk.

Investigating topics and issues together.

Negotiating real purposes for writing.

Giving opportunities for reflection.

Teachers' Notes 1

GETTING IDEAS AS A GROUP

Aims:
1. To help children get ideas for writing.
2. To stimulate discussion.

Objectives:
1. Taking the children through the procedure for gathering ideas and organizing thoughts.
2. To use talk as a means of making the ideas clearer.

Group size: individual/pairs/groups (maximum of three).

Timing: 15–30 minutes depending on age of children.

Organization:
1. Groups need to sit close together for the discussion and so that all can see and contribute to the brainstorm chart.
2. Any kind of group as appropriate.
3. Adult to act as scribe for the group if writing is difficult.

Resources: Photocopied Sheet 1 for planning – one per group or one for each individual; a large sheet of paper for demonstration.

What to do:
1. Introduce the class to the brainstorm idea by getting them to help you do one on a large sheet of paper.
2. Let them try one for themselves.
3. Discuss results in the course of the work as well as at the end, either as a class or in groups.

Cross-curricular links: it can be adapted to any area. This process is particularly suitable for story-writing and planning projects.

Follow-up activities/extensions:
1. Children can number the ideas at the end of the arrows to show in which order they will organize them for their work.
2. Very young children or less confident writers can put their ideas down in picture form.

Photocopiable Sheet 1

GETTING IDEAS AS A GROUP

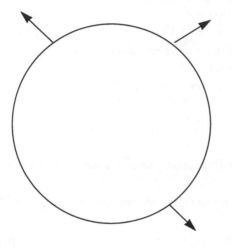

1.   Make a list of three topics/areas of interest:
     a)
     b)
     c)

2.   Put your ideas about what you want to find out at the
     end of the arrows.

3.   Choose the arrow you want to find out about most.

Teachers' Notes 2

LOOKING BACK/LOOKING FORWARD

Aims:
1.   To encourage reflection upon the process of writing.
2.   To highlight co-operative group skills in the process of writing.
3.   To encourage learning from experience.

Objectives:
1.   To develop the ability to communicate opinions and feelings.
2.   To share individual accounts and insight.
3.   To use talk and writing to help organize what the pupils want to say.
4.   To develop confidence in speaking about one's work to an audience.

Group size: individual/pairs/small group/whole class.

Timing: 30 minutes.

Organization: groupings as thought most appropriate. Teacher could act as scribe for one group at a time.

Resources: Photocopiable Sheet 2 for planning – one per group or one per pupil.

What to do:
1.   Talk through the headings with the children so they are aware of the purpose of the work.
2.   Encourage them to think of issues which relate both to what they produced and to how they worked together.
3.   Discuss issues which keep coming up as a whole class and invite individual groups to share their thoughts.

Cross-curricular links: this task can be adapted to any area in the curriculum.

Follow-up activities/extensions:
1.   Note matters which arise in the groups: these can be worked on by the whole class, e.g. how do we make a decision when there are several good ideas?
2.   It can be used with some adaptations for children to evaluate a term or a year's written work on an individual basis.

Photocopiable Sheet 2

LOOKING BACK/LOOKING FORWARD

1.   What has the group achieved?

2.   What do you feel pleased about?

3.   What difficulties did you come across?

4.   How did you try to cope with the difficulties?

5.   Think of three things which people said which really helped the group to work well:

   a)

   b)

   c)

6.   Think of two points in your work when talking with someone else helped you to succeed:

   a)

   b)

7.   What do you think *you* could do next time to support the group more?

Teachers' Notes 3

PLANNING A REPORT

Aim: to help pupils to develop a logical approach to reporting back to the class some aspects of group work they have been engaged in.

Objectives:
1.   To work collaboratively to produce a verbal report.
2.   To listen to and put forward opinions and insights.
3.   To learn to communicate effectively within a small group and to a larger audience.
4.   To learn how to plan.
5.   To learn how to organize ideas through writing.
6.   To use writing to help remember ideas.

Group size: maximum of four.

Timing: 30 to 60 minutes for first two sections, 30 minutes for the final two sections.

Organization:
1.   Groups need to be able to sit close together for the discussion.
2.   Any kind of grouping which is seen to be appropriate.

Resources: Photocopiable Sheet 3 for planning – one per group; extra spare paper for notes.

What to do:
1.   Go through the headings, discuss what is meant by them and what the pupils need to talk about.
2.   The first two sections can be completed in the first session if desired.
3.   The third and fourth sections will need completing on separate occasions.
4.   Encourage groups to share their thinking and views after each session.
5.   Share difficulties and successes during the course of the sessions.

Cross-curricular links: applicable to any area.

Follow-up activities/extensions:
1.   Once used to the structure, the pupils should be able to do this kind of planning without the sheet.
2.   Tape-record the reports which the groups give, then discuss with the pupils the effectiveness of the communication.
3.   Ask the pupils if the planning sheet helped them at all: could they devise a better one?

PLANNING A REPORT

The thinking stage
Discuss as a group what the main points are which you want to include in your report.
Jot them down here:

The organizing stage
In what order do you think the points should be presented?

Decide who will: introduce the report;

talk about the different points;

show pieces of your work.

What else do you need to organize? Note ideas below:

The trying-out stage
Try out the report. Discuss what happened. Note any changes to be made.

Evaluate after the event
Make notes about how the group feels after the report has been presented. What will
the group concentrate on next time?

INVESTIGATING AN INSECT

Aim: to produce an information book about an insect chosen by the pupil/group.

Objectives:
1.   To produce well-organized writing.
2.   To use forms of writing appropriate to task.
3.   To encourage careful presentation of work.
4.   To encourage planning with others and evaluating outcomes.

Group size: two to four pupils.

Timing: four to six hours spread over a period of three days.

Organization:
1.   Groupings as thought most appropriate.
2.   Provision of space for working with a large number of resources.
3.   Can be done as a whole class, or a few groups can work on the books while other pupils are occupied in other tasks.

Resources
1.   Photocopiable Sheet 4 for planning – one per group or one per pupil.
2.   Access to a wide selection of books; careful planning of resources by the pupils will alert the teacher as to what will be required.
3.   Variety of writing tools, paper and means of 'publication'.

What to do
1.   Talk with the pupils about the possible subjects they might choose;
2.   Talk through the purposes of different parts of a reference book as a reminder;
3.   Discuss the importance of working through the order of planning as described on the sheet.

Cross-curricular links: this activity can be adapted to any area of the curriculum.

Follow-up activities/extensions:
1.   Develop the first editions into hard-back copies for the school library or a class reference section.
2.   Make reference books for younger children to supplement their work or story books for the younger classes using their ideas.
3.   Gain the views of the effectiveness of the books by testing them out with other classes; hold a debate in which the readers can offer constructive criticism for the writers.

Photocopiable Sheet 4

INVESTIGATING AN INSECT

1. Think of an insect you would like to find out about.

2. Write here the questions you have about the insects to which you want to find answers. You should think of at least six questions:

   a)

   b)

   c)

   d)

   e)

   f)

3. Find books to help with your answers.

4. Make notes about the answers you have found. Collect these in a folder to use for drafting your work.

5. Now begin to make a reference book about your insect. It should have:
   - illustrations and writing;
   - a front cover;
   - an index and contents page;
   - a list of the books you have used (bibliography).

You may work with a friend to produce the book.
You should aim to produce a book of quality, showing detail, care and accuracy.
Your book will be added to the non-fiction library collection.

Chapter 6

Story-telling in the Classroom and Across the Whole School

Mark Prentice

Mark Prentice is an experienced primary deputy headteacher. His interest in developing children's speaking and listening led to his being involved in the National Oracy Project (1988–1991). The work described here focused on using story books to promote children's talk and on exploiting the potential of story-telling, with different groups, from pairs to the whole school.

BACKGROUND

I first realized the power of story-telling in developing children's learning through my encounters with the technique of 'teacher in role'. With this technique, the teacher can structure and influence dramatic experiences for the children, without breaking the imaginative spell of the characters which the children have adopted. For example, if the children are reconstructing a scene or story from the Civil War, the teacher might step into the play/action as a passer-by who saw the Cavalier troops setting up camp, or as an informer or a wounded Roundhead in disguise. Through the intervention, the children might be encouraged to consider deeper psychological factors, create new twists to their improvised plot or recover the thrust of the action if they had started to drift into detail or irrelevance.

My interest in role-play and drama widened to include the art of story-telling, which is at the heart of the oral tradition. Like drama, story-telling is about bringing stories alive through the interaction between teller and audience. In order to develop children's story-telling skills, children have first to experience a wide range of stories, both written and oral. The more teachers tell stories to children, the better they become at learning how to capture the children's attention with the tone of voice, facial expressions and body language. The children emulate these techniques and experiment with them when sharing stories with each other.

Children are constantly making sense of their world through stories, or relating their own experiences or fears to those found in stories. For example, during the development of the whole-school story, described below, a group of children decided that one of the main characters, a red monster, had a bad tooth due to eating too many rich people. Some children talked about their own teeth and tooth fairies, other children discussed the issue of decay and the juicy details of the monster's rotten tooth. An older child seized upon this idea to move the plot of the story forward. If the villagers found a way of getting rid of the monster's bad tooth, would the monster stop attacking the village in return? A discussion followed about the biblical saying 'an eye for an eye and a tooth for a tooth' and the moral basis of our story.

Telling stories to and with children can help them to discover themselves. Children can rehearse feelings and situations, and indirectly prepare for the challenges and conflicts which lie ahead and which, invariably, feature in good stories. They can experience alien and hostile worlds within the safety of listener or reader. They can discover times, places and people that differ from their familiar contexts and thereby widen their understanding and imagination. Every story has a structure of some kind which provides order for the ideas and events. It may be claimed that by learning to appreciate the structured world of the story, the child learns to make connections, identify patterns and impose order upon his own experience.

AIMS

This chapter looks at the use of story-telling in the classroom and as a whole-school approach. It has two central aims:

- to illustrate how you can develop children's story-telling skills through activities in the classroom;
- to describe the creation of a whole-school story, which can generate a sense of enthusiasm, excitement and involvement in children.

The chapter is designed to help teachers to:

- encourage children to have an understanding and love of story-telling;
- develop children's story-telling skills;

- help children to become more aware of audience and enhance their confidence when telling stories to others;

- increase a child's awareness of the difference between the spoken and written word;

- help children develop, through narrative, their emotions, intellect and imagination.

STARTING OUT

In the classroom

Before embarking upon a whole-school story-telling project, it is clearly advisable for individual teachers to involve the children in a variety of story-telling activities in the classroom. There are several activities suggested in the Programmes of Study for English.

The following activities may also be useful in developing story-telling skills in the classroom. They can be adapted to suit most age groups and topics, and may provide some helpful guidelines for planning and organization:

ACTIVITY BOX 1

Stories in the round
The children retell a familiar story. They could do this in the round, where one child starts the tale, the next person follows on, and so on until all the children have participated.

ACTIVITY BOX 2

Story rhythms
Again, the children retell a familiar story but they step in and out of a circle in time to a rhythm, chanting or clapping as they echo each individual's contribution.

Ch. 1:	There were three brown bears
Class:	There were three brown bears
Ch. 2 :	Who lived in the woods
Class :	Who lived in the woods
Ch. 3:	They went for a walk one day . . .

ACTIVITY BOX 3

Story ingredients
The children identify and discuss story elements:

- Characters or creatures which represent the conflict between good and evil.
- A trick or trickster.
- A place; the story setting.
- Repetition of language patterns or events (note: the number three occurs frequently in fairy tales).
- A journey.

After discussing the ingredients of a good story, the class can then devise their own group story to tell.

ACTIVITY BOX 4

Storyboards
Children outline a story plot, using the key elements which have been discussed. This helps them appreciate story structure.

You can use *Photocopiable Sheet 1* for the children to record their ideas.

ACTIVITY BOX 5

Multi-media story-telling
There are infinite ways to retell stories for an audience. Children enjoy using different techniques and approaches.

- OHP: visual images are projected to support a story told to a larger audience.
- Drama: the story-teller, freed from the need to read, can be encouraged to support the tale with gesture, movement, voice modulation and sound effects. The audience can mime actions or provide sound effects, when prompted by an agreed cue.
- Dance: groups of children can use dance to tell a story or parts of a story.
- Puppetry: simple figures made of card or fabric can be used to act out a story. Shadow puppets are particularly effective.
- Art: 2-D and 3-D work can support the story-teller as prompts and enhance understanding for the audience. Figures moved along a frieze, pictures in sequence, papier maché landscapes are just a few examples of the way art and oracy can be linked.

ACTIVITY BOX 6

Whole-class story-making

The children work in groups. Each group nominates a scribe and a spokesperson. The children generate ideas and feed back to the class. Links are identified and the different groups' ideas interwoven to make a single story.

When creating a group story in the classroom, it is helpful to establish a basic set of rules for the children to observe.

- One person speaks at a time.
- Establish eye contact.
- Try to follow on what a person has said, or challenge his/her point of view in order to develop the story.
- There is no right or wrong. There are many different ways of telling the same story and each story-teller brings something of him- or herself to a story.

Across the school

It was to further develop story-telling skills with children who were familiar with story-telling in the classroom that led to a whole-school story-telling project in a Buckinghamshire first school. Children from each class collaborated to create a fairy tale about a monster which was then performed to the school and local community.

The project offered an exciting vehicle for communicating to parents the value of oracy across the curriculum. The children provided the content of the project while the teachers devised activities which developed skills outlined in the Programmes of Study for the National Curriculum. The initial stimulus for the project was carefully planned.

1.   There was an in-service day involving local story-tellers and artists working alongside teachers to explore different ways of developing stories. The children's interest in story-telling was stimulated by a performance of *Sir Gawain and the Loathly Lady* which incorporated puppetry and music with story-telling.

2.   Each class-teacher then focused upon British folk tales for two weeks. Folk tales are particularly effective for telling and retelling because their story-lines are predictable and they invite audience participation through their rhythmic and repetitive patterns. Folk tales also speak to all levels

of the human personality and engage children's imaginations through fantasy. Each class decided, by negotiation, which aspect of folk stories they would like to study in depth. The six classes chose monsters, dragons, giants, knights and chivalry, magicians, spells and words, and story landscapes and settings.

3.   Over a period of five weeks, twice a week, two children from each class came together to create a story from the ideas they had developed in their separate classes. After each story session, the children had to tell the story as it had evolved so far, to their classmates. The children also had a problem to solve which they had to bring back to the next story session. Through the collaboration of older and younger pupils and the contributions of each class, the school worked together to create our own unique tale.

MOVING ON

Whole-school story sessions were organized along the following lines: two children from each class in the school came together to create a story, using the ideas they had developed in their separate classes. The teacher acted as chair person, helping the children reach co-operative decisions.

PHASE ONE

Each pair of children was introduced to the rest of the group as experts from their field of study or story feature.

T: 'These two children know all about dragons . . . Could you tell us what you have learned . . . ?' Tell us more about your own dragon . . .

Ch: 'He's big, scaly, green but when he blows fire, he shrinks . . . He used to frighten people but he doesn't any more.'

Very soon, a picture of our story elements emerged. The recipe for a good opening was discussed. It was agreed that the story should open with a 'bang', a red monster crashing through the forest . . . 'blood, excitement, people being eaten . . .'

The group decided, however, that if the monster ate everyone, the story would be over too quickly. Listening to the children negotiate their ideas for the story provided a great deal of useful evidence about their oracy skills. At the end of each session, we reflected upon the part of the story that we had created. Each pair of children had to return to their class and tell the story so far.

PHASE TWO

Each pair of children was given a problem to solve that was relevant to their story element. The children were asked to solve this problem within their class and bring a solution to the next story group meeting, e.g.:

Dragons: how could the dragon help the villagers?

Magicians: how could a magic spell change the monster?

PHASE THREE

After a day or two, the story-making group met again, but this time there were twice as many children, each pair bringing another pair from their class. The core group (first group) told the story so far and then returned to the classroom. The second pair discussed the problems and how their class had decided to solve them and then worked on the next part of the story. This process was repeated, enabling several children from each age group to be involved. In this way, a complex story grew through word of mouth as each day, children discussed the latest developments. In the classrooms, each teacher further developed their own story elements. One school assembly per week was also dedicated to sharing together how the story was taking shape.

IN FULL SWING

The performance

The project led to several specific outcomes and provided a variety of ways to evaluate the children's achievements. The children created a book of the story with the teachers acting as scribe. They illustrated this and it was printed by students from a local secondary school. Every child took a copy home to read to their parents. Many parents reported their child's enthusiastic response to the project. The children wanted to read and reread the book, and discuss ways in which their class had contributed to the story.

For the performance, it was agreed that each class would take responsibility for acting out the part of the story which featured their particular element most strongly. The plot was held together by one group of children who narrated the story.

The story was performed several times, with music, dance, song, artwork, puppets (including a huge red monster with a movable jaw), OHP scenery, lighting and special effects.

Each performance captivated the audience and children alike. Overall, the event appeared to be highly successful in raising the profile of story-telling and oracy across the school.

Evaluation

At the weekly story sessions, I analysed and assessed the children's story-telling skills and followed the development of interactive dialogue between the children in the group. During these review sessions I was not looking for right or wrong answers, but the ability of the children to discuss ideas and to be able to reason and debate with each other. As the whole-school story was being created, the following frameworks for assessing children's ability to discuss stories proved useful.

Background information using contextual clues:

- Tell me who you think lives here? Who inhabits this landscape?
- Can we tell what sort of monster this is? How could we categorize these characters?
- What is going to happen next? What would be surprising or predictable?

Issues relevant to the particular story:

- How did these characters come to be together?
- How do they feel?
- Why are they as they are? e.g. beautiful or ugly, jealous, scared?
- Who is brave in the story?
- Which characters change? Why?

Issues that relate to story-telling in general:

- Why are stories often frightening?
- What is the difference between fact and fiction?
- Is a story ever real?
- Whose story is it? The characters'? The author's or the story-teller's?

The skills and processes of story-telling:

- What do story-tellers do with their hands?
- How important is the audience's reaction?
- How can story-tellers use their voices to hold the audience's attention?

Collecting evidence

Clearly, it is useful for you to collect evidence of children's developing story-telling skills, for example:

- Through using a tape recorder: this provides you with evidence of attainment. Also children can listen to the tape and discuss it together or with you.

- Through using a video: watching themselves on film enables children to reflect on their non-verbal habits and skills.

- Through observation: while observing the group you can note who is dominating the discussion, who is competent at summarizing what has been said. An evaluation sheet for recording story-telling sessions can be found on *Photocopiable Sheet 4.*

Monitoring oracy activities involves identifying the skills which need to be developed, devising activities which will require those skills, and recording whether children are moving forwards. The list of *story-telling skills* on page 105 can be used to provide a framework for reviewing specific activities.

Ted Hughes once called stories 'little factories of understanding'. When creating their own stories, children can be encouraged to invent new ideas based on their previous experiences. When children create their own stories they demonstrate 'Some of the more powerful abstract concepts that we ever learn – good/bad/love/hate/fear/security and so on. They use abstract concepts to make sense of concrete content' (Kieran Egan, 1988).

In the creation of the whole-school story, the children were encouraged to explore universal moral and philosophical issues. For example, they debated whether the villagers could trust the monster to be their friend now that they had helped him.

For staff and students, the project made possible a new relationship between the teachers and the taught. The whole-school story grew out of collaborative effort. It was passed from child to child and from child to adult orally, thereby involving the children in the traditional process of story-telling.

STORY-TELLING SKILLS

1. Retelling a known story.

   - Can retell a tale with help from adults or props.
   - Can retell a tale using simple sentence structures and vocabulary.
   - Can retell a tale using more complex sentence structures, images and phrases.
   - Can retell a tale confidently using tone of voice, accents, feelings, facial gestures and body language.
   - Can retell a tale using all the above and also elaborate upon the original plot using own ideas.

2. Telling own story: the above skills can be related to a child's own story.

   - Can use imagination to devise original plots, characters and outcomes.
   - Can devise surprise endings, twists to plot, etc.
   - Can adapt stories to suit audience responses.

3. Listening to stories.

   - Can listen attentively and respond to others' oral stories, in pairs, small and large groups.
   - Can listen attentively and respond to stories read aloud.
   - Can identify different kinds or genres of story through listening.
   - Can recognize and identify different dialects or accents when encountered in stories.
   - Can detect subtleties of meaning from the speaker's intonation and tone, e.g. sarcasm, irony.

4. Talking about stories.
   - Can discuss own experiences in relation to a story which has been told.
   - Can give and defend opinions about a story.
   - Can describe feelings stimulated by listening to a story.
   - Can discuss story-lines, characters and outcomes with confidence.
   - Can discuss language features used by the story-teller.
   - can discuss audience reaction to a story told aloud.

(Note: the same list can also be used for assessment purposes.)

KEY POINTS

Start out by valuing every contribution made by a child.

Time and space to tell stories are needed.

Offer support within the group, but guide only where necessary.

Right or wrong? Help children develop tolerance.

Independence of ideas and confidence are goals.

Encourage a shared wish for the advancement of ideas.

Stories at school, stories at home . . . stories for telling and discussion.

Teachers' Notes 1

STORYBOARD

Aims/Objectives:
1. To enable children to create their own storyboards as a stimulus.
2. To tell their own stories.
3. To enable children to work collaboratively.
4. To encourage children to sequence a story.

Group size: whole class or a group (six to eight). Pairs of children can work together to create a storyboard, or individual children can work on their own storyboard.

Timing: half-an-hour to an hour. The children need to come back to this activity several times in order to produce quality work.

Organization: use Photocopiable Sheet 1 as an idea. The sheet can be enlarged onto A3 size paper. Alternatively, mark out squares for the children on large pieces of card or sugar paper. Children will be able to create and mark out their own storyboards using rulers.

Resources: Photocopiable Sheet 1, felt pens, crayons or pencils. Provide a variety of media for creating a collage.

What to do:
1. Encourage the class to brainstorm the elements of a 'good' story. Discuss the ingredients of stories.
2. Scribe the pupils' ideas onto a large sheet of paper or a blackboard.
3. Encourage the children to make up their own story using these elements, working in small groups or in pairs. Allow plenty of time for this.
4. The pupils then draw their ideas on an individual storyboard. They have to sequence their story giving it an exciting beginning, a middle section and a resolution (some pupils may need two storyboards). Encourage the pupils to write words or captions under their pictures.

Cross-curricular links: Technology: developing and communicating ideas.
English: talking in groups, talking about their own texts, audience awareness, reading for meaning, interpreting texts, storywriting.
Art: illustrating stories.

Follow-up activities/extensions:
1. Using their storyboards, pupils can tell their story as a puppet show using the overhead projector (see page 110).
2. Create a puppet show using puppets made from sticks and card or glove puppets.
3. Tell their story using the storyboard. A tape recorder can also be used.
4. Retell someone else's storyboard story.
5. Write the story.
6. Create a three-dimensional landscape model which tells the story and provides a setting for the story.
7. Turn the storyboard into a board game using dice, i.e. go forward two, chased by the monster.
8. Cut up a photocopy of the storyboard to use in a sequencing task.

STORYBOARD

Name:		4.		8.
Date:		3.		7.
		2.		6.
Title of story		1.		5.

Teachers' Notes 2

THE LAMBTON WORM

Aims:
1. To introduce the pupils to Old English and dialects.
2. To encourage pupils to develop speaking and listening skills in responding to a text.

Objectives:
1. Listening with attention and concentration.
2. Investigating how language varies.

Group size: whole class, small groups.

Timing: 30 minutes

Organization: discuss different dialects and how language changes over time. Explain you will read a traditional poem which comes from the North East. It may be helpful to introduce some key words in the poem, e.g. bairns, heuk, fash, hoyed.

Resources: Photocopiable Sheet 2 and, written on cards, some examples of words in the poem, the meaning of which children can attempt to guess.

What to do: read and discuss the poem with the children. Divide the children into small groups and assign each group a part of the poem. They can then retell the story of the Lambton Worm in modern English (standard or your own local dialect). When each group is ready they will be asked to share their verse with the whole class. The modern verses could be tape recorded for transcription at another time.

Cross-curricular links: history.

Follow-up activities/extensions:
1. The children could write out their modern version of the Lambton Worm and display it alongside the traditional one.
2. When you have finished you might like to retell a picture book story in a dialect or in 'olde fashioned Englishe'.
3. Discussing the Lambton Worm as outlined in this chapter (discussing stories).
4. Analysing dialects, i.e. the class can identify words from the poem which differ from standard English or other dialects, e.g.

Lambton Worm (verse 1)	Standard English	Other
morn	morning	marnin'
heuk	hook	'ook
hyem	home	'ome
whisht	quiet	shhh

THE LAMBTON WORM

The Lambton Worm
One Sunday morn young Lambton
went a-fishin' in the Wear;
An' catched a fish upon his heuk.
He thowt leuk't varry queer.
But whatt'n a kind of fish it was
Young Lambton couldn't tell.
He waddn't fash to carry it hyem.
So he hoyed it in a well.

Chorus:
Whisht! lads, haad yer gobs.
Aa'll tell ye aall an aaful story.
Whisht! lads, haad yer gobs.
An' Aall tell ye 'boot the worm.

Noo Lambton felt inclined to gan
An' fight in foreign wars.
He joined a troop o' Knights that cared
For neither wounds nor scars.
An' off he went to Palestine
Where queer things him befel,
An' varry seun forgot aboot
The queer worm i' the well.

Chorus

But the worm got fat an' growed an' growed.
An' growed an aaful size:
He'd greet big teeth, a greet big gob,
An' greet big goggle eyes.
An' when at neets he craaled aboot
To pick up bits o' news.
If he felt dry upon the road,
He milked a dozen coos.

Chorus

This fearful worm wad often feed
On calves an' lambs an' sheep,
An swally little bairns alive
When they laid doon to sleep.
An when he'd eaten aal he cud
An' he'd had he's fill
He craaled away an' lapped his tail
Seven times roond Pensher Hill.

Chorus

The news of this most aaful worm,
An' his queer gannins on,
Seun crossed the seas, gat to the ears
Of brave an' bowld Sir John.
So hyem he cam an' catched the beast
An' cut 'im in three haalves.
An' that seun stopped he's eatin' bairns
An' sheep an' lambs and calves.

Chorus

So noo ye knaa hoo aal the folks,
On byeth side of the Wear,
Lost lots o' sheep an' lots o' sleep
An' lived in mortal fear.
So let's hev one to brave Sir John
That kept the bairns frae harm.
Saved coos an' calves by myekin' haalves
O' the famis Lambton Worm.

Chorus

---

hoyed – threw; gan – go; senn – soon; coos –
cows; swally – swallow; cud – could; bairns –
children; knaa – know

Teachers' Notes 3

THE LAMBTON WORM SLIDE SHOW

Aims:
1. To encourage pupils' story-telling skills.
2. To sequence a story.

Objectives:
1. Ages 5 to 10 years.
2. Listening in order to respond to texts: awareness of genre (i.e. poetry and prose).
3. Talking about texts.
4. Audience awareness.
5. Knowledge about language.

Group size: whole class or groups of six to eight within the class.

Timing: half-an-hour per session.

Organization:
First session: The teacher talks to the group about dialects, possibly playing a tape with examples of people speaking in different dialects. The pupils then listen to the teacher reading the poem and are encouraged to ask questions about the text.
Second session: Pupils draw their version of the sequence of the Lambton Worm on the slide.
Third session: Finishing off and making the frame.
Fourth session: Telling the story to an audience.

Resources: a copy of the poem. An enlarged (A3) version of the sheet, preferably on card; felt pens, pencils or crayons. It may be necessary to simplify and explain the poem.

What to do
1. The pupils can make their slide on card.
2. The pupils draw their version of the Lambton worm, sequencing the story in the six sections.
3. They cut out the slide.
4. The pupils cut out the frame and place it over the slide.
5. The pupil moves the slide along each section as they tell the story of the Lambton Worm to a partner.

Cross-curricular links: technology: planning and making. Art and design: investigating and making.

Follow-up activities/extensions:
1. Pupils making their own slide shows for their own stories.
2. Writing a script for their slide show.
3. Creating a puppet show or OHP show of the Lambton Worm.
4. Pupils telling their story to different audiences (i.e. parents, other classes, assembly, etc.).

This is a very effective way of showing a story.

Photocopiable Sheet 3

THE LAMBTON WORM SLIDE SHOW

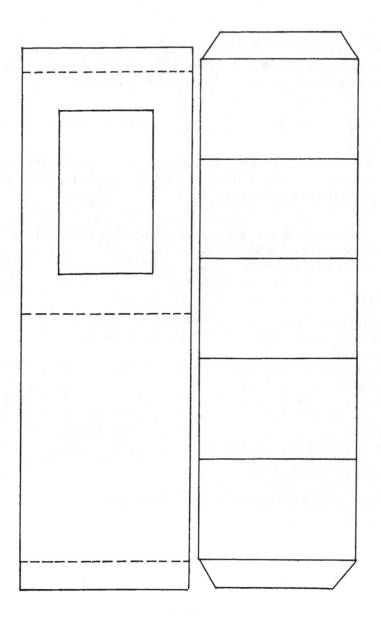

Teachers' Notes 4

EVALUATION SHEET FOR STORY-TELLING AND LISTENING TO STORIES

Aim: to assess which level of attainment the pupils have reached in Speaking and Listening.

Objectives:
1. Telling stories.
2. Using language appropriate to a role or situation.

Group size: up to twelve children may be involved in the group discussion. However, when assessing the children it is best to focus upon four children at a time.

Time: up to half-an-hour.

Organization : the teacher needs to be with the group. The rest of the class could be engaged in other activities.

Resources: a story to discuss. Perhaps one that the children have created or a story book with layers of meaning and good illustrations that will inspire the children to discuss them, e.g. books by Anthony Browne or David McKee.

What to do:
Discuss issues within the story with the children using the four phases of discussion:
1. Background information using visual and contextual clues.
2. Issues relevant to the particular story.
3. Issues that relate to story-telling in general.
4. Reflections on the skills and processes of story-telling.

It is important to establish agreed ground rules for yourself and the children.
- Value every contribution made by a child, and guide comments back towards the group for discussion.
- Encourage the children to address, challenge or agree with each other directly, not via the teacher.
- Always maintain that there is more than one point of view to be experienced.
- It is also valuable to consider how you can assess the group discussion.
- These sessions can be tape recorded to help analysis of dialogue.
- It is important to take notes while observing the group discussion.

Follow-up activities/extensions:
1. Draw pictures or talk about the group discussion.
2. Create a poster identifying good story-telling characteristics.

EVALUATION SHEET FOR STORY-TELLING AND
LISTENING TO STORIES

NC Level	Teacher's evaluation	Pupil's comments	Pupil's name	Date	Stimulus	NC Focus

Chapter 7

Developing Oracy Through Drama

Suzi Clipson-Boyles

Suzi Clipson-Boyles is director of the Catch-up project and a senior lecturer at the School of Education, Oxford Brookes University, where she teaches English, drama and early years education. She has a broad experience of teaching across the full age range and her drama work with primary pupils has been featured on radio and television. She has written various publications in the field of language and literacy, including drama.

BACKGROUND

When considering all the ways in which oracy activities might be planned for primary school children, drama is one of the more obvious choices. However, there is still the belief amongst some that drama is primarily about reading or acting plays. There is no doubt that using scripted texts and performing created stories can be a useful facet of oracy work, but this way of working represents only a fraction of the potential which drama has to offer.

In primary education we are not in the business of training children to be actors. However, we should be aiming to provide meaningful interactive contexts for learning, and drama is an appropriate and effective medium for that purpose. Drama is not so much a subject to be taught, but perhaps more importantly it is an approach to learning. It is a means by which children can explore ideas and experiences through a whole range of methods and styles of teaching. Not only can these methods be used to teach about language, they can also be employed to deliver rich learning experiences which relate to other areas of the curriculum.

Drama might feasibly be described as a natural extension of children's play which can be carefully structured in order to maximize the educational opportunities. It is this exploratory and experiential aspect of educational drama which distinguishes it from 'theatre'. Inevitably, there are occasions where performing to each other is an appropriate part of the work, but it is more often the processes which have led up to that product which offer the most value in terms of children's learning.

A report published by HMI (1990) identified the value of drama very clearly, saying that: '. . . *the teaching of drama has a strong influence upon the development of language and literacy . . .*'

However, the inspectorate were disappointed to note that: '*Only a minority of primary schools have a well-developed policy and guidelines for their work in drama. Consequently drama rarely receives consistent attention either as a means of enriching work in other subjects or as an activity in its own right.*'

It is hardly surprising that drama was considered to be a 'luxury' item at that time. In the early 1990s, teachers in England and Wales were preoccupied with the delivery of the new and overloaded National Curriculum. Due to the sheer pressure of such intensive reforms, pedagogical issues tended to be put on hold, and there was a move towards content delivery through more formal methods, hence the scarcity of drama in the majority of schools inspected.

Now that teachers feel more familiar and comfortable with the 'slimmed-down' curriculum content, they have started to return to the teaching methods which they know are effective in relation to children's natural ways of learning. Drama is one such method, and if more reassurance is needed to authenticate the inclusion of drama in the primary curriculum, one only has to refer to oracy in the National Curriculum for permission. Drama is statutory requirement for speaking and listening.

The purpose of this chapter is to explore some of the ways in which these requirements can be delivered successfully.

AIMS

The specific aims of the chapter are to:

- assist planning for oracy development through drama;
- explore ways of incorporating drama into the oracy curriculum;
- explore different approaches to drama in the primary school;

- offer guidelines for the organization and management of drama;
- show how aspects of the National Curriculum can be delivered through a creative and active approach to learning;
- offer examples of good practice in developing oracy through drama.

STARTING OUT

Drama can provide appropriate and meaningful contexts for children's learning across all subject areas, and in doing so becomes an excellent vehicle for an oracy curriculum. However, it can be helpful to use a framework for planning. One such model is illustrated here:

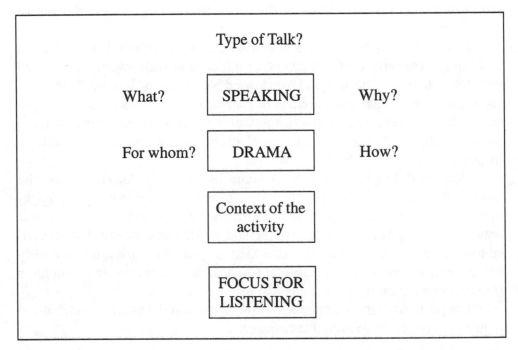

This model may provide a useful check-list for planning. For instance, the following example shows how the model was used to map out the beginnings of a lesson in which the teacher wanted the children to work on the listening to and following of directions.

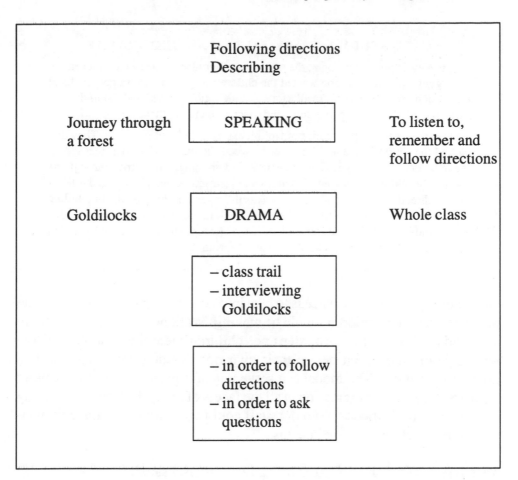

The following Case Study demonstrates how this framework can support young children's learning of geographical terms through actually using them within a drama context. It is good example of children learning by modelling on an adult, exploring new knowledge and revisiting it in a variety of ways. In this particular example we can see:

- demonstration;
- imitation;
- exploration/experimentation;
- application;
- revision.

CASE STUDY 1: FAIRY TALES AND GEOGRAPHY

In this Key Stage 1 classroom, the teacher used guided imagery and hot seating for a geography lesson. She wanted the children to practise using geographical terms, in particular 'river', 'road', 'forest', 'hill', 'up', 'down' and 'behind'. Key skills included following directions and description using those terms.

The teacher read the two stories of Goldilocks and Red Riding Hood. They discussed the similarities and differences between the two stories, then focused on the location. In the playground, the teacher led an imagined journey through the forest. The children followed her actions and instructions which included following the directions listed (e.g. wading across the river, climbing up the hill, hiding behind the trees when the wolf came, etc.). Back in the classroom, she pretended to be Goldilocks and invited the children to ask her questions using the terms and directions they had been practising in the playground.

Good quality planning also needs to take into account the larger picture of the progression which children should be making. Work needs to be sequentially arranged if it is to build step by step upon children's learning in a constructive way. Schools will often devise their own policies and approaches to this aspect of planning. The model can serve a useful purpose here by enabling teachers to consider progression in all the facets of oracy. For example, taking the top box on the model ('Type?'), staff could consider following a sequential guide which might look like this:

Year 1	Term 1	Exploring ideas in discussion.
	Term 2	Developing ideas in discussion.
	Term 3	Considering more than one possibility.

A systematic approach such as this ensures a broad but progressive coverage of an oracy curriculum which enables teachers to focus, concentrate and consolidate skills in real depth. Of course, this should not, nor cannot, eliminate other types of talk from taking place. In the following Case Study, we can see how older children worked on a quite complex project in which they had to research, plan, design, write, present and evaluate. Although the main focus for evaluation was the presentation of information to an audience, other types of talk also, inevitably, took place.

CASE STUDY 2: WORLD WAR TWO

This teacher used imagined mime sequences followed by spontaneous improvization to explore the key concepts of evaluation from city to country and the effects of World War Two on people's lives at home. Other key skills included finding information, organizing and presenting ideas.

Having read about and discussed the reasons and procedures for evacuation during World War Two, the children had a drama lesson in the hall exploring air raids, leaving home, and arriving in a strange place. The pupils then worked in groups of eight to present a newsreel feature. This included narration, interviews and snapshots of scenes (for example, children boarding the train in London, picnics in the country, etc.). A large news-plan of the sequence was devised as part of the planning process and scripts were written for each section. The differences in use of language were also considered (e.g. narration versus action shots). The final pieces were performed to the rest of the class and evaluated by all.

By developing a well-structured framework for long-term and short-term planning and progression we can ensure that:

1. our planning is guided;

2. we have continuity between terms and between year groups;

3. we have a clear focus for our evaluations;

4. we are building upon developmental foundations for learning because the work is appropriately sequential;

5. we have a thorough and systematic approach to the oracy curriculum.

MOVING ON

A variety of approaches

Having decided what the children need to learn, we then have to choose the most appropriate and effective ways of planning and delivering the activity. This involves four main components for consideration:

1. the form of drama;

2. group size;

3. space;

4. time.

1. The form of drama

There are many forms of drama which can be selected. The main ones are listed below, with a guide to the particular opportunities offered for oracy within each. They are listed in a particular order, moving from freer-flowing experiential activities towards approaches which require the children to do more planning and preparation.

*   *Guided imagery*: the teacher talks through an imagined sequence which the children play through as she talks and they listen.

    Example: exploring a beach, finding shells.

*   *Mime*: a situation is presented through actions and facial expression but without speech. However, speaking can be a useful part of the planning process.

    Example: planning to perform a well-known fairy tale in mime for others to guess.

*   *Movement*: creating moods, shapes or moving pictures.

    Example: exploring the changing moods of the sea and illustrating its dangers and its pleasures.

*   *Tableaux*: the children make picture scenes (sometimes called 'freeze frames'). These can be individual or linked as a sequence, joined by movement, narration, music, poetry, etc.

    Example: use non-fiction books to research Viking funeral rituals then present in tableau form.

*   *Role play*: taking the role of another character, real or imagined. Role play can be set into many contexts, spontaneous or rehearsed.

    Example: younger children playing in home corner, playing out the roles of adults.

*   *Spontaneous improvisation*: in-role exploration of an idea without any forward planning. The outcomes are not necessarily determined.

    Example: during a family meal a phone call is received to say they have won £100,000.

*   *Interviewing*: one partner is in role and the other partner interviews them either in role or not.

    Example: one partner in role as a parent arguing in favour of school uniform.

- *Hot seating*: one character is in role and is questioned by the class, or by a smaller group. The person in the hot seat could be the teacher, a visitor or one of the pupils.

  Example: children research evacuation in World War Two then go into the hot-seat to be questioned by the rest of the class.

- *Simulated experience*: similar to spontaneous improvization, this technique is to enable the children to go through a pre-planned experience. The difference is in the preparation, discussion and more structured framework. The teacher often works in role with the children.

  Example: arriving at an airport with check-in desks, cafés, shops, passport control, etc.

- *Reconstructed improvisation*: having done an initial spontaneous improvization, they then go back over it and start to refine it into a more shaped piece.

  Example: taking the previous example, they would then consider how the story would unfold, develop and end.

- *Story shaping*: this can be a follow-on from some of the methods already mentioned, or it can be used after discussion, research or stimulus starting points. The children brainstorm ideas, then organize them into story sequence for live presentation.

  Example: after preparative research, the children construct a story about one day in the life of a child living in Ancient Greece.

- *Script reading*: reading commercial scripts or scripts which they have written themselves provides children with a rich opportunity to read for meaning. The stage directions alone can result in marvellous debate and interpretation.

  Example: having read scripts (with stage directions) about conflict, the children plan for basic performance (i.e. with movements planned and parts rehearsed but not learned by heart).

- *Script writing*: this is usually most effective after an exploratory activity so that the children already have material with which to work. It is important to show and explain examples of actual scripts so that they can learn about the format and compare it with direct speech in prose. Let the children exchange with another group so that they can read it.

  Example: the children could take one section of a story to translate into script form (one minute of talk can take more than an hour to write!).

- *Staging*: the true spirit of educational drama is about experiences rather than acting. However, where appropriate contexts are used and the children are fully involved in the planning, design and delivery of a performance, there is much learning which can take place.

  Example: presenting a simplified version of 'A Midsummer Night's Dream' could involve the children in writing, oracy, technology, art and history in addition to the obvious reading development opportunities for exploring and enjoying Shakespeare

2. Group size

Group sizes can make an enormous difference to the quality of children's work. Pair work is useful in the classroom situation where an interactive activity is required in limited space. Case Study 3 illustrates an example of this.

CASE STUDY 3: NEWSPAPERS

This teacher wanted the pupils to develop their skils in questioning and in describing events. They had already done some work on Standard English and a range of talk for different purposes.

In the classroom, each pair looked at a local newspaper together. They eventually selected a story which interested them and read this through two or three times, making notes where necessary. They then went into role, one child playing the part of a newspaper journalist, the other a character from the story.

Evaluation took place with another pair. They took turns observing each other and gave feedback based on their questioning techniques and the detail of their descriptions.

Working in threes can be usefully employed, particularly when one child is the observer and gives feedback.

Sometimes the children will work in larger groups and such whole class drama is both exciting and fruitful. The golden rule is to consider the appropriateness of group size every time we plan, so that the children can experience variety, and that the working possibilities match our expectations.

3. Space

Space, or rather lack of it, is often used as a reason for not doing drama. But not all drama requires a large space. Pair interviews can take place in the classroom at tables. Miming and guessing can be a whole-class activity, for example eating particular things in different ways as an introduction to science work about food. It is also worth considering using one area of the classroom for small group work during the day when other activities are also taking place at the same time. For example, setting up a role play area of a police station or optician's with activity cards, writing materials, and dressing-up clothes can prompt some worthwhile opportunities for speaking and listening which could then be followed up by other work.

4. Time

Time is arguably the most precious commodity available to teachers, and the one which most commonly runs short. With careful planning it is quite possible to provide learning experiences which provide valuable oracy opportunities through drama whilst teaching different areas of the curriculum. It is quite valid to spend twenty minutes in the hot seat as a character such as Marie Curie in order for the children to ask questions at the end of a science research session.

Drama does not always have to constitute a grand large-scale event or even a whole lesson. Very often quick five-minute spontaneous role play can provide an extremely good stimulus introduction to another topic.

IN FULL SWING

Assessment

Once the drama is in full swing, there is much to do in terms of assessment, recording and reporting. Because in oracy work we are very much concerned with skills in action, it is vital to observe the processes of the work as well as the end product or 'performance'. Much of this will be on an informal and intuitive level, but there will also be time to make more planned assessments of children's work. In my experience, once the children are working independently they are usually so absorbed in what they are doing that it is possible and practical to make close observations and records.

This section discusses some approaches to these different aspects of evaluation and reflection in drama.

Informal observation and intervention

The nature of drama is organic and sometimes unpredictable, so it needs to be watched, nurtured and occasionally pruned or assisted. In order to do this we need to observe and listen constantly – a kind of 'tuning in'.

The following questions provide a mental check-list of the sorts of things we need as we walk round the classroom:

- Is everyone on task?
- Has everyone understood the instructions?
- Do any groups need additional information?
- Should I make any changes to my original plan?
- Are they going to have enough time?
- Is the talk purposeful?
- Do I need to intervene?
- Shall I intervene in role?
- If they finish quickly, what else can extend their thinking?

Formal assessment and recording

When planning for drama, it is not only important to identify clearly the points for assessment, it is also necessary to plan how and when the observations will take place.

The following five-point plan outlines simple guidelines for formal assessment of oracy during drama:

1. Know what is being assessed.
2. Plan what will be seen as evidence of competence.
3. Inform the children of what is expected of their work.
4. Ensure that any record keeping reflects progression.
5. Feed back to the children.

Feeding forward and reporting back to the children

If children are going to recognize and value drama as a valid part of their learning programme, we have to give them consistent messages which make this clear. This is an ongoing part of the communication process. This might include comments such as the following, made before, during and after a lesson with Year 2 children. They had planned and presented an alternative story for well-known characters of their choice from traditional tales:

FEEDING FORWARD AND FEEDING BACK

Feeding forward:
I will be watching carefully to see if you are taking turns to speak during your discussions . . .
Make sure that everyone suggests at least one idea . . .

Comments during:
I like the way you have changed Red Riding Hood into a bad character.
That is going to make the story very different.
Don't forget to try different voices for each character . . .

Reporting back:
I liked the way this group wrote down each idea before choosing . . .
This group nearly quarrelled at the beginning, and Anna made the excellent suggestion that they should put their hands up when they had something to say. Well done, that group!

In other words, we need to highlight those skills which we are hoping to develop and give them high status in our discussion with the children.

Children's reflections and evaluations

It is also important to demonstrate to children that not only do we value their comments, but that they are actually a part of the work to be done. Evaluations become more effective through being clear about what is to be the assessment focus. The children's own reflections upon their achievements also benefit from guidance, otherwise there is a danger of wasting time on bland comments which reflect little critical analysis. The following suggestions are intended to offer a framework for children's evaluation processes:

- Before watching the work of others, we need to guide their thinking. Example: 'While you are watching this group, take note of two facts about the Victorians which you think they discovered in their research.'

- Encourage them to ask each other questions after watching each other's work. Example: 'I would like you to think particularly of questions about the way they worked in their group.'

- Build variety into the evaluation process. Example: Feeding back to a new partner, written comments, suggestions for change, etc.

- Constantly reassure the children that it is all right to admit that they made mistakes, or could have done something better, because this honesty reflects mature and constructive thinking. Example: 'Now that you have agreed that the story didn't have a very strong ending, tell me what you would do differently if we had time now.'

KEY POINTS

Doing, being and thinking through a variety of approaches.

Reflecting upon experience.

Action, interaction and involvement.

Mapping out the lesson and planning carefully.

A richness of contexts for oracy.

Teachers' Notes 1

SURGERY ROLE-PLAY CORNER

Aims:
1. To enable children to assume roles in imaginative role play.
2. To assess children's speaking and listening.

Objectives:
1. Talking for a range of purposes.
2. Describing imagined events.
3. Talking within specific roles (doctor, receptionist, nurse, patient).

Group size: whole class for 'Simon Says' and discussion; maximum of three at any one time in role-play corner.

Timing: 15 minutes for 'Simon Says' and discussion; 20 to 30 minutes maximum in role-play corner.

Organization: the role-play corner should be set up in the classroom, although this might mean rearranging the current format. The role-play session should be planned so that all children get at least one turn on a systematic basis. This could mean twelve children per day.

Resources: the role-play corner should include a receptionist's desk with office equipment (telephone, paper, pens, appointment book, etc.), leaflets, magazines, doctor's area with two chairs, desk, bed, posters, eye chart, scales, prescription pad, stethoscope, etc. Dressing-up clothes are always an asset, but avoid stereotyping through provision (e.g. only female nurses' uniforms).

What to do:
Discussion back in the classroom about the parts of the body. What job do they do? Where are they joined? What happens if you fall? etc.

1. Play 'Simon Says' as follows: you instruct the children to use various parts of the body (e.g. 'Simon says show me your elbows'). However, when you say 'Show me your elbows' the children must freeze and not obey your instructions. If they do respond they are out of the game.

2. Introduce and discuss medicines, highlighting the dangers and the uses, perhaps showing examples of medicine bottles, drug packets, etc.

3. Explain about the role-play corner. Discuss three roles in detail: receptionist, doctor and patient. Importance of describing accurately, listening carefully and giving instructions. Each child should take a turn at all three roles.

Cross-curricular links: science (understanding of science in health contexts).

Follow-up activites/extensions:
1. Label selected parts of the body on own drawing.
2. Invent a medicine to make you happy.
3. Find story and information books with pictures of hospitals, doctors and nurses.

Photocopiable Sheet 1

SURGERY ROLE-PLAY CORNER

Assessment Sheet

Half-term:_____

Child's name	Turn taken	Named parts	Explained drugs	Talked in role

Teachers' Notes 2

WORKING IN THE MILL

Aims
1. To explore some aspects of the lives of Victorian orphans and child mill workers.
2. To enable children to respond to and reflect upon the drama.

Objectives:
1. Participating in role play and drama, sharing ideas, insights and opinions.
2. Using language appropriate to a role or situation.
3. Discussing and planning ideas with others.

Group size: whole-class introduction; groups of six to develop own stories.

Timing: 20 minutes whole-class section.
            20 minutes smaller group work.
            20 minutes showing and evaluating.

Organization: the children will already have done preparatory work on factory conditions and workhouses. This should be through discussion, video material, and the use of non-fiction activities.

Before starting the session in the hall, ask the children to lay out two rows of chairs (about eight in each row) upside down to represent mill machinery. Place these at one end of the hall in the 'mill area'. The other side of the hall will represent the 'workhouse area'.

Resources: large hall space; chairs which can be turned upside down; cymbal and beater (or hand bell if possible); large white apron for the teacher to wear as the workhouse mistress; top hat and/or cloak for the teacher to wear in role as the mill owner; large cushion to sit on when wanting to come out of role.

What to do:
1. Explain that you are all going to pretend to be in the workhouse, and later the mill. You will join in as the workhouse mistress when you wear the white apron, and the mill owner when you wear the cloak and hat. It is important for the children to understand that when you sit on the 'Time Cushion' you are all back to the present and that is your signal for them to gather around you to discuss what they have done so far.
2. Ask the children to find a space and lie on the floor, close their eyes and relax. You should then talk them through an imagined scene (guided imagery). This might include descriptions of the workhouse where they are sleeping, wooden floors, broken windows, damp walls, rats, no blankets, sound of crying, hungry stomachs, no toilets, etc. Tell them that when they hear the cymbal (or bell) they should reluctantly get up to go for their gruel and water, before starting work. It is 4.30 a.m. . . .
3. Give them time to think about this and get into role, then you go into role yourself as the cruel mistress, shouting, ordering them up and into the eating area where you will dole out the gruel.
4. After they have 'eaten their gruel', sit on the Time Cushion and discuss what has happened so far. How did they feel, what did they think, what else might you add to the scenario? If appropriate, you could run the scene again, adding any suggestions from the children. The next stage is to walk the long journey through the snow and wind to

---

Teachers' Notes 2 (continued)

---

the mill. Lead this out of role, talking them through an imagined journey. Eventually, they arrive at the mill where you can go into role as the owner who is waiting to shout at them for arriving late. They set to work immediately, working the machinery under instruction (e.g. 'You boy! Pull that shuttle through faster! Faster, I said!').

5. Again, come out of role to discuss the mill scene. Ask for suggestions (e.g. someone might get caught in the machinery). Replay.

6. Go back to the beginning and run through one more time.

7. Now, in groups of six, the children should be asked to work with those basic ideas to develop stories of their own. They should consider the characters in more detail, giving them names, ages, a brief history. They need to think of the order of their story – it doesn't necessarily need to begin in the workhouse for instance. Allow them to improvise and explore their ideas for ten minutes, then ask them to start shaping them into a story which is more planned to show the rest of the class.

8. Allow each group to show their story. (If time is short, have three groups at each end of the hall so that they show to half of the class simultaneously.) Ask the children to notice the ways in which the performing groups are speaking. How did they change the way they were speaking to represent the characters they were playing (e.g. vocabulary, accent, volume, appropriate tone etc.)?

Cross-curricular links: history (the Victorians).

Follow-up activities/extensions: the children could write scripts of their stories. Photocopiable Sheet 2 invites the children to write guided diary extracts.

DIARY OF A MILL CHILD

My name is:

This diary describes my feelings when . . .

. . . I had to get up at 4.30 a.m.

. . . the cruel mill owner hit the children

. . . there were accidents in the mill

. . . we were given bread as a special treat instead of gruel

. . . at the end of the day

Teachers' Notes 3

THE GREAT LEISURE CENTRE DEBATE

Aims:
1.   To enable children to speak for a specific purpose and audience.
2.   To enable children to empathize with contrasting points of view.
3.   To consider the complexity of planning and developing land.

Objectives:
1.   Presenting and listening to features of an argument.
2.   Using spoken language within a formal context.

Group size: groups of four for the preparatory research; whole class.

Timing: 10 minutes introduction; 20 minutes preparatory research (10 minutes individually followed by 10 minutes in groups of four); 30 minutes simulated meeting.

Organization: after an initial introduction to the whole class, the children will work at their tables, firstly on their own, followed by ten minutes in groups of four. The room should then be arranged for a meeting. This often works best with the children sitting at tables around the edges of the room in a square shape facing the middle.

Resources: one copy per child of Photocopiable Sheet 3: 'Leisure Centre . . . Yes or No?', large sheets of sugar paper, chunky felt tips, large plan of the proposed site (perhaps relating to your own local environment if that is appropriate), dressing-up clothes (optional), flip-chart with a plan of the proposed site.

What to do:
1.   Discuss the reasons why planning applications are legally necessary.
2.   Show the children your large plan of the proposed leisure centre which will include four cinemas, tropical swimming pool, two restaurants and bowling alley. Try to make this sound absolutely wonderful, but also quite controversial, for example, building it on fields, new busy road, knocking down old theatre, etc. It would be particularly effective if you could design your plan to fit into your actual local environment. Discuss the pros and cons briefly, then introduce the idea that views will vary according to who you are. Ask the children which groups they could represent at a public meeting: e.g. younger residents for, older residents against, environmentalists, builders, planners, councillors, etc.
3.   Having sorted them into the groups, give them ten minutes to reflect individually on their photocopied sheet. They should then work in groups to plan their campaign. They should share their initial ideas on a large sheet of sugar paper (one per group) about how they would feel, and 'facts' which they could bring to the meeting. They should also plan who they are, how old they are and then go on to practise in their groups how they are going to speak in the meeting.
4.   Arrange the room for the meeting, assemble the children, then go into role as chair of the parish/town or city council. Thank them for coming and announce that this public meeting has been arranged to give people the opportunity to express their views about the proposed plans for a new leisure centre which will include four cinemas, tropical swimming pool, two restaurants and bowling alley. Take a vote at the beginning and

end of the meeting. Run the meeting formally, addressing them by their last name (i.e. 'Mrs Smith would like to speak . . . ') and insist on turn-taking. It is important, however, to allow them to disagree and argue sometimes in order to develop a realistic atmosphere (like the House of Commons) but this should be in role and not allowed to get out of control.

Cross-curricular links: geography: appropriate geographical terminology to describe and interpret surroundings (planning, site, development); consideration of local features, their effect upon the environment, and human activity.

Follow-up activities/extensions:
1. Write a report of the meeting for a local newspaper.
2. Write a letter, in role, expressing your views on the proposals to the council.

LEISURE CENTRE . . . YES OR NO?

As you will have read in the local papers, the _____Council have received planning application from FUNFUN DEVELOPMENTS LTD to build a new leisure centre at _____.

The Council invites you to make your views known on this survey sheet.

Thank you.

Name_____

Age _____

Occupation_____

Photograph

Why leisure centre should be built	*Why leisure centre should not be built*
1.	
2.	
3.	
4.	

How will the leisure centre most affect you?

IN THE NEWS

Aims:
1.　To consider and practise styles of presenting information.
2.　To organize material for presentation.
3.　To analyse critically items of real news.
4.　To encourage children to read beyond the text.

Objectives:
1.　Exploring, developing and explaining of ideas.
2.　Reporting, describing events and observations.
3.　Presenting to an audience.
4.　Reading newspapers for information and inference.

Group size: six children per group.

Timing: two hours (could be split into two halves)

Organization: 15 minutes introduction with the whole class; 45 minutes planning in groups in the classroom; 1 hour putting plans into action, plus performance, in larger space.

Split the children into TV news teams (maximum six per team). Encourage them to choose a name for their channel.

Resources: five different national papers from the same day carrying the same story. One photocopy of the Editorial Planning Sheet (Photocopiable Sheet 4) per group. Two local newspapers per group.

What to do:
1.　Introduce the children to the idea of different representation of the same story by showing them the national newspaper examples. For obvious reasons, it is best to avoid political stories.
2.　Ask the children how documentary-type news items are presented on television by identifying typical features (e.g. introduction, narration, action shots, experts, two opposing views, etc.).
3.　Explain the activity as follows: they should look at the local newspapers and choose one story to present as a television feature. However, rather than presenting just the information printed in the article, they should imagine what else might have happened as part of the story. They should also consider if they want to present a range of views (e.g. fox hunting), or make a strong point about a particular issue (e.g. abolition of the fur trade).
4.　They should use the Editorial Planning Sheet to finalize their plans. They can write the names or roles of two experts, e.g. fireman/teacher and the opinions expressed. They can then identify the action shots and choose one journalist for their group to actually present the broadcast. The other five children can represent one film shot each as a freeze-frame when presenting their broadcast to the rest of the class.
5.　Once the planning sheets are completed, the children will need to improvise the scenes and explore the language of the presentation. This should be done in the hall. Once they are happy with the format they should start to finalize what will actually be said in the final version by making quick scripts.
6.　The class should watch each group and discuss the bias or balance after each.

Follow-up activities/extensions: the scripts could be written up as film scripts, then given to other groups to read aloud.

IN THE NEWS

Editorial Planning Sheet

Expert 1	Expert 2	Opinion 1
		Opinion 2
Action shots		Journalist

Filming plot:

Shot 1 _____ **Shot 3** _____

Shot 2 _____ **Shot 4** _____

Chapter 8

Philosophical Discussions with Picture Books

Karin Murris

Karin Murris has an international and national background in developing children's philosophy and critical thinking. The author of the teacher's manual, *Teaching Philosophy with Picture Books*, she uses story books, already in schools and popular with children, to foster philosophical discussions. She has worked with many schools, universities and LEAs, running workshop sessions on enhancing children's critical and creative thinking.

She recently completed her PhD in teaching philosophy to primary school children. She has been trained under Professor Matthew Lipman at the Institute for the Advancement of Philosophy for Children (IAPC), Montclair State College, New Jersey, and is recognized as a trainer by the International Council for Philosophical Inquiry with Children.

BACKGROUND

In the late 1960s Matthew Lipman, Professor in Philosophy at Columbia University in the USA, was struck by his college students' incapacity to express themselves creatively and critically. As a result, Lipman devoted the rest of his career to developing and distributing his 'Philosophy for Children' programme. The idea of the programme is for children to read aloud together from a purposely-written philosophical novel. The children then discuss what they (and not the teacher) find puzzling and interesting in the story.

The teacher's role is to help the children make a 'community of philosophical enquiry'; this is successfully achieved only when all participants work non-competitively together by using each other's ideas as building blocks to form beliefs that are more accurate or balanced. The teacher is helped in this difficult role by teachers' manuals consisting of exercises, games, discussion plans, etc., for extending the children's thoughts and arguments.

Lipman's method of using the community of enquiry is typically Socratic in form. It was the ancient Greek philosopher Socrates – the central character in Plato's earlier dialogues – who saw education as a continuous quest, of endless speculation with a focus on questioning, rather than answering pre-set questions. When thinking Socratically, people discover that they cannot easily define ideas that are central to the beliefs they often hold with such certainty. This ignorance in turn inspires authentic curiosity and critical reflection upon one's own thinking and experiences.

AIMS

The aim of this chapter is to share this passion for thinking with others by introducing some of the core ideas of philosophy to children. Philosophical discussions will encourage children to:

- feel confident about their capacity to think for themselves.
- think more critically and creatively.
- be more tolerant and less prejudiced.

STARTING OUT

Why picture books?

Although my method is quite similar to Lipman's, in that it is Socratic, we differ mainly in our ideas about the best educational materials with which to start a philosophical discussion. I prefer to use existing children's stories. Authors of good children's picture books have a rare talent for combining artistic skills with an ability to engage children's sense of fun and imagination.

So many stories exist that are not only entertaining, but also very well written and thought-provoking (either text or illustration, or both). Therefore, not only is there no need to write novels especially for the teaching of philosophy, it is also more economical for schools to make better use of existing resources.

Using picture books also offers easier access to ideas for a greater number of children, especially those with special educational needs. Lipman's 'Philosophy for Children' programme starts off with children taking turns in reading aloud a few sentences of the novel. I have noticed that many poor readers are so nervous about reading their passage 'properly' that they fail to listen to what the others are reading, and miss the philosophical ideas in the story. Of course, they are allowed to 'pass', but this will emphasize their sense of failure.

Picture books easily provoke discussions about life, death, freedom, friendship, time, space, animal rights, right, wrong, good, bad, etc. The children often generate the philosophical ideas as a result of a tension between the 'not-real' (what happens in the story) and 'real' life. For example, in the picture book *The Pig's Wedding* by Helme Heine, two pigs – madly in love – are standing on a cloud. It is impossible to stand on clouds, nine-year-olds in one of my philosophy classes thought, and they went on to discuss what kind of material clouds are made off. To be able to stand on clouds, clouds must be solid, but if clouds are solid they would fall down and crash onto the ground. On the other hand, how do we know clouds are not solid? 'Well,' one child argued: 'aeroplanes go through them, and if they were made of ice, aeroplanes would have *ice cream* wipers, and not *windscreen* wipers!'

The main advantages of using good quality picture books to teach philosophy are:

- they are rich in thought-provoking, sensuous images and powerful ideas;
- they are often funny and imaginative;
- they are short, entire stories (ideal for one-hour discussions);
- they are pictorial (ideal for young readers, or children with reading problems).

Picture books make stories readily accessible. The television may offer even easier access. Recently, many good quality picture books have been made available in *audio-visual* format, which adds the following advantages to merely using the book:

- *all* children in large mixed-ability classes are easily involved;
- despite different reading abilities, all children can share a story-experience;
- seeing stories is ideal for children whose intelligence is more visually orientated;
- children may get used to being more thoughtful about what they watch on television;
- videops/films and CD-roms may encourage reluctant readers to pick up books and read them by themselves afterwards.

MOVING ON

The approach in practice

Central to the approach is the role of the teacher, who uses questioning to encourage the children to challenge their own and other people's thoughts.

CASE STUDY 1: WHERE THE WILD THINGS ARE

The following transcript is of a group of five- and six-year-olds discussing the famous picture book, *Where The Wild Things Are*, written and illustrated by Maurice Sendak. It consists of short parts of a much longer discussion in order to show the line of reasoning. The children are seated in a circle. They have contributed questions about the story, which I have written up on a flip-chart, as follows:

1. Max must have been dreaming. (Tim)
2. Why did he go to the monsters? (Tammy)
3. Why was his Mum angry? (Katie)

The picture book features some monsters (the Wild Things), and we enter the discussion just after Tim remarked that Max must have been dreaming.

Ben:	'I agree with Tim, because there is no such thing as monsters.'
KM:	'How do you know?'
Ben:	'Because . . .'
Tim:	'You've never seen one.'
Ben:	'You've never seen one.'
KM:	'So, because you've never seen monsters, there *are* no monsters. What do you think of that thought?'
Kerrie:	'There is no such thing as monsters, because . . . mmm . . . there was a long time ago, but now they've all died out.'
KM:	'So they *did* exist, but now they don't exist any more.'
Kerrie:	'Only in places, there are only bones of monsters, there you can see there were monsters a long time ago.'
KM:	'So the bones are evidence that they did exist?'
Kerrie:	'When I went on the see-saw I found a bone.'
Michelle:	'You can't get real dinosaurs, you can only get pretend dinosaurs . . . you have to wind them up, and then they can walk.'
KM:	'What I'm trying to understand . . . does it mean that all the things we have never seen . . . ?'
Michelle:	'It doesn't mean that there is no . . .'
KM:	'What do you mean, Michelle?'
Michelle:	'It doesn't mean there is no dinosaur.'
KM:	'Why not?'
Michelle:	'There might be some.'
Heather:	'There might be some in zoos.'
Kerrie:	'There might be some a long way from here, and they don't come here.'

KM: 'So although we have never seen a monster, doesn't mean they don't exist. Is that what you are saying?'

Kerrie: 'There might be some a long way away, and they don't come here, because they might be too frightened.'

Tim: 'I don't agree with Kerrie, because there is no monsters, no dinosaurs anymore, 'cos they were only in the days that there weren't any people.'

KM: 'So how do we know that something exists?'

Jonathan: 'Well, you can't get dinosaurs, but you *can* get camels . . . in the desert, but not dinosaurs.'

Kerrie: 'Well, some of them might just lay eggs and they might just leave them there, and they might go somewhere else and *they* might die, but the little baby ones might still be alive *now*, and they might be still in a different country.'

Rebecca: 'I agree with Kerrie.'

KM: 'Could you explain why?'

From this excerpt it can be seen that the children that day touched on the philosophical problem of how it is that we know that something exists. Kerrie originally believed that dinosaurs do not exist, but the thinking of others made her change her mind and she came up with the creative thought that it could have been the case that they had laid eggs, and baby dinosaurs could be alive somewhere else without us knowing it! (Their speculative play with ideas took place before Steven Spielberg's *Jurassic Park* was in UK's cinemas.)

Planning for learning

The children in the transcript above were not merely talking, but they were engaged in a *philosophical* discussion. How can we tell the difference, and how can we achieve the same with our pupils? Some key elements to look out for in philosophical discussions:

1. Are the children clear in expressing their thoughts? e.g. Michelle: 'It doesn't meant that there is no.' I asked, for example: 'What do you mean, Michelle?' But I could also have asked: 'What are you saying?', 'Could anyone help her?'

2. Are the children giving reasons for their beliefs? Rebecca, for example, gave the following reasons: 'Well, *because* they might be frightened of us, *because* they might think we'll begin to kill them.' I asked, for example: 'Why not?', 'How do you know?', 'Could you explain why?' I could also have asked: 'Do you have any reasons for saying that?'

Are the children defining concepts? Are they classifying, categorizing concepts? In another discussion, I asked, for example: 'Was Max day-dreaming or dreaming, and what is the difference?' Other questions could have included: 'What does it mean to exist/think/dream?'; 'How many kinds of thoughts are like dreams?'

4. Are the children able to change their viewpoint? Kerrie believed at first, that all dinosaurs have died out, but Michelle's idea made her think about other possibilities. The teacher could ask: 'Do you disagree with what you said before?', or, 'What made you change your mind?'. Children changing their mind is a very good sign in a discussion. It tells us they are listening to each other, but also are open to persuasion based on arguments – they are open-minded enough to change their opinions.

5. Are the children hypothesizing and speculating? Kerrie, for example, said: 'There might be some a long way away, and they don't come here, because they might be too frightened.' I asked: 'So the bones are evidence that they did exist?' Further questions could be: 'What if . . ., what could happen?', or, 'Now, suppose that . . . ?'

6. Are they listening to and building on each other's ideas? They said, for example: (Michelle): 'There might be some'; (Heather): 'There might be some in zoos'; (Kerrie): 'There might be some a long way from here, and they don't come here' – a good example of how they were extending each other's thoughts. I said, for example: 'What do you think of that thought?' It might be helpful to ask: 'Who agrees with x?', or 'Have you anything to add to x's idea?'

The teacher's role as a *facilitator* is crucial in philosophical discussions. We have to listen carefully to what the children are saying, and if thoughts are not clear to everyone, they will need to be clarified (preferably by the same child, possibly with the help of the other children). We also have to provoke their thinking further by asking questions. We should, however, *never* answer their questions ourselves. What we personally think is not important, because if children realize that we own the discussion, they will ask the sort of questions, and give the kind of answers, they think we expect from them. It is absolutely essential that the children decide the topic and the course of the discussion. We should never be directive. Instead we should be prepared to follow the enquiry wherever it may lead.

The children should feel responsible for how the discussion is going. We can try to encourage this by not saying anything when there is a moment's silence. Thinking time is a good thing and will also put the emphasis of the discussion more on the children, and less on us.

Or, we could steer the children to assume greater responsibility by asking certain questions, such as: 'Which of your questions and remarks do you prefer talking about best?', or 'Could someone answer her/his question?'

Discussions will never be philosophical if the teacher herself is not puzzled by the sort of questions that could be raised. If the teacher has an open-minded attitude, then children's questions will stimulate the teacher's own thinking. Philosophical questioning is an expression of wonder about ourselves, the world, and other beings – to be perplexed about the world as it *is*. One of the great benefits is that children will start to think about their own thinking, because they will think about what they say, how they say it, and what others say.

Praise children when they express opinions they have thought out themselves.

When teaching Socratically, the *only* tool allowed to be used in this process (for children and adults alike) is that of reflection on experiences that in principle are accessible to all. It is important therefore that neither the children nor the teacher are allowed to refer to 'authorities', such as big brothers, Mums or Dads, books (not even encyclopaedias), or statistics.

IN FULL SWING

Planning for organization

The same picture books can be used for children as young as three and as old as eleven. I have found an hour's discussion per week is about right. The children can spend as many weeks as they want discussing just one picture book. For example, a class of ten-year-olds spent many weeks on discussing the 'easy' picture book *Changes, Changes* by Pat Hutchins. Its apparent easiness masked a wealth of philosophical enquiry. The story has no text at all, and features as the main characters two wooden dolls in problem-solving situations. One of the questions the children discussed was the question they raised themselves: 'Why can human beings make decisions and not wooden dolls?'

Each age group will use the same story in a different way, but there are some basic organizational principles which are advisable. Organize the class in such a way that everyone can see and hear each other well – a circular setting is best, with or without desks. Start the lesson by showing the video of a picture book, or reading the story aloud. Subsequently, allow a few minutes of thinking time by asking the children to write down what they find puzzling, or interesting to talk about. Then they discuss their thoughts in pairs for another couple of minutes. Their questions or remarks can then be written on a large piece of paper next to their names, and be kept for next time. The group chooses one topic for initial discussion, e.g. 'What makes a person bad or good?' We can help to guide discussions with questions, such as:

- Is it bad to steal?
- Is it bad to steal food when you are starving?
- How many bad things do you have to do to be a bad person?
- How many good things do you have to do to change from a bad into a good person?

Try to bring each session to a close, for example, by a last round of comments, or a discussion in pairs, or a summary of the discussion either by the facilitator, or by one of the children.

A following session might start off with watching the video again of the same picture book, or just reading the book out aloud, after which the previous week's remarks are read from the sheet of paper. A topic is chosen, and the discussion can begin or continue where it left off the previous week. Each picture book could lead from discussion into other areas of the curriculum. One school spent many hours, after discussing *Where The Wild Things Are,* on making a forest in a corner of the classroom, designing 'Wild Thing' masks, and acting out the Wild Rumpus in PE.

Planning for review

The most effective way of evaluating philosophical discussions is taping or video-taping the sessions. It will show the progress children are making. We can look out for the following:

- They are listening to each other/following the discussion.
- They respect the procedures of the discussion.
- They are more confident in sharing their thoughts with others and participate more in the discussion.
- They understand questions better.
- They give reasons for their beliefs.
- They give individual and original answers.
- They direct their questions and answers at the child(ren) involved and not at you.
- They use each other's ideas as 'building blocks'.

- They discover connections between concepts.
- They are critical of what happens and analyse the characters in the story.
- They can defend a particular point of view.

Wider benefits

Apart from the cognitive skills children will acquire, many teachers have noticed children showing more *care* in the classroom. They may display more understanding and respect for their classmates, and more tolerance generally.

When interviewed by Channel 4's 'Class Action' in November 1994, ten-year-olds told the viewer: 'With philosophy you can express your feelings', 'Philosophy has helped me to talk in class', 'You think again about things', 'You might think that philosophy is easy and maths is hard but you have to use your brain', 'You don't have to write anything, the only time when you draw is when draw it in your mind', and 'In philosophy you can change your mind . . . that's good, because you think of more ideas'.

Research carried out by the Welsh Office and published in 'Improving Reading Standards in Primary Schools Project' shows gains for Year 1 pupils in: thinking and reasoning; listening skills; expressing language; discussion and debating skills; confidence and self-esteem.

Key Stage 1
Pupils should:

- explore ideas;
- use talk to develop and clarify their thinking and extend their ideas in the light of discussion;
- relate stories to their own lives and experiences, and to draw upon these experiences when talking about the story;
- ask questions which clarify their understanding of an account, and to answer questions in ways which indicate a thoughtfulness about the matter under discussion;
- reflect, respond to or extend the ideas and opinions of a previous speaker.

Key Stage 2
Pupils should:

- talk to explore, extend or trace the logic of an idea, discuss to find things out and to share accounts or insights;

- make exploratory and tentative comments when ideas are being collected together and reasoned, evaluative comments as discussion moves to conclusions or actions;
- listen carefully to others, questioning them to clarify what they mean and extending and following up the ideas;
- begin to qualify or justify what they think after listening to other opinions or accounts and deal politely with opposing points of view.

For children with special educational needs: For pupils who may have learning difficulties in reading and writing, it is the oral outcomes that will, perhaps, provide the main basis for thinking about experiences, expressing feelings and engaging with society.

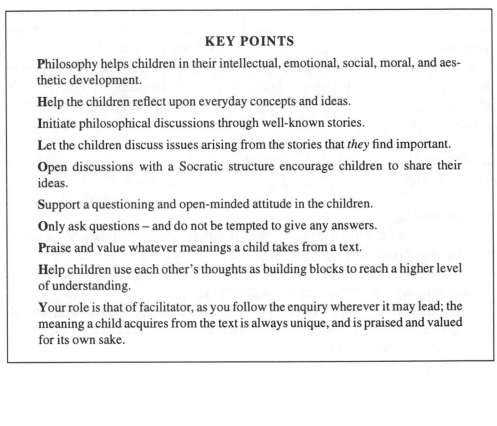

KEY POINTS

Philosophy helps children in their intellectual, emotional, social, moral, and aesthetic development.

Help the children reflect upon everyday concepts and ideas.

Initiate philosophical discussions through well-known stories.

Let the children discuss issues arising from the stories that *they* find important.

Open discussions with a Socratic structure encourage children to share their ideas.

Support a questioning and open-minded attitude in the children.

Only ask questions – and do not be tempted to give any answers.

Praise and value whatever meanings a child takes from a text.

Help children use each other's thoughts as building blocks to reach a higher level of understanding.

Your role is that of facilitator, as you follow the enquiry wherever it may lead; the meaning a child acquires from the text is always unique, and is praised and valued for its own sake.

FOOD FOR THOUGHT

Aim: to encourage children to think about thinking.

Objectives:
1. Discussing traditions relating to food.
2. Considering the viewpoint of a stranger.
3. Performing a role play.

Group size: minimum of eight; maximum of 35.

Timing: 15 minutes.

Organization: normal classroom setting.

Resources: pencils, photocopies, pencils, something to write/draw on.

What to do: give each pupil a photocopy of Photocopiable Sheet 1. Ask them what they think the dog could be thinking of. They can write or draw four different options in the thought-bubbles. In groups of four they can then share and discuss their dog's thoughts with each other. Each group decides on the best thought within their group. Finally call the class together and collect the thought-bubble from each group, display these and ask the groups to generate questions about the possibility of dogs being able to think these thoughts.

Cross-curricular links: science, design and technology.

Follow-up activities/extensions: (minimum of one hour)
1. Show a picture of an English Sheepdog thinking of sausages. Discuss what is meant by the expression: 'Food for thought', 'You are what you eat.' Ask the children to give more examples of expressions with food in them.
2. Divide the class into groups of four. Ask the children to imagine the following situation. As a family they are sitting at the table eating their Sunday roast. When they are tucking into their Yorkshire pudding and roast beef, suddenly out of nowhere a strange creature from outer space lands next to their table. Fortunately, this creature speaks and understands English. The creature asks them what it is they are eating, why this and not something else?

   Encourage them to think of as many aspects of the situation as possible, e.g.: Why eat meat? Why eat in the afternoon? Why with knife and fork (with manners generally)? Why cook our meals differently in different countries? What is 'good' food?

   In their small groups they first of all discuss what the conversation between the alien and the 'family' is going to be like. One of them writes the dialogue down, while others make quick cartoon-like illustrations.

   Let them act out the conversation that develops between the alien and the 'family' in small groups, after which they can perform for each other. Afterwards, they can make a drawing of the situation.

FOOD FOR THOUGHT

The dog in Jenny Wagner's book *John Brown, Rose and the Midnight Cat* did a lot of thinking.

'He thought all through lunchtime and when supper came, he was still thinking.'

Draw, or write down what this dog is thinking.

Teachers' Notes 2

QUESTIONS: THINKING

Aim: to encourage children to think more clearly about their own thinking.

Objective: justifying their beliefs and listening to their peers.

Group size: minimum of eight, maximum of 35.

Timing: minimum of one hour.

Organization: four tables facing each other and separate from other groups of tables.

Resources: Photocopiable Sheet 2, scissors, a 'hat'.

What to do: divide class into groups of three; cut the photocopy in strips and put them in a 'hat'; a representative of each group takes one strip, on which there is one question. Each group reads out aloud its question, then *all* groups try to answer this question in the small group, after which they share their ideas in the large group. Subsequently, the second group reads out aloud their question, etc.

Cross-curricular links: Personal and Social Education (PSE).

Follow-up activities/extensions: read out aloud the following poem and discuss. Ask the children to make up their own poem.

> YOU ARE OLD, FATHER WILLIAM
>
> 'You are old, Father William,' the young man said,
> 'And your hair has become very white;
> And yet you incessantly stand on your head –
> Do you think, at your age, it is right?'
>
> 'In my youth,' Father William replied to his son,
> 'I feared it might injure the brain;
> But now that I'm perfectly sure I have none,
> Why, I do it again and again.'
>
> (Lewis Carroll, *Alice in Wonderland*)

Photocopiable Sheet 2

QUESTIONS: THINKING

----

1. Does thinking *hard*, make you think *better*?

----

2. Are you *always* thinking?

----

3. Can you think without a brain?

----

4. Can you run out of thoughts?

----

5. Are a dog's thoughts like human thoughts?

----

6. Is it possible to think without words?

----

7. Do computers think the way we do?

----

8. Do bad thoughts make you a bad person?

----

9. Do your thoughts belong to you?

----

10. Are thoughts like little television screens in our head?

Teachers' Notes 3

THE THINKING GAME

Aim: to talk about thinking.

Objectives:
1.   Discussing and justifying their beliefs.
2.   Agreeing and disagreeing with their peers in a structured way.

Group size: minimum of eight, maximum of 35.

Timing: one hour

Organization: semi-circular classroom setting around a blackboard on chairs only.

Resources: Photocopy, Blu-Tack, blackboard, scissors.

What to do:
1.   Cut photocopy in small strips along the dotted line.
2.   Distribute the statements evenly among the children, who then discuss the statements in pairs. Do they agree or disagree with the statements?
3.   When the discussion in pairs takes place, you make three columns on the blackboard with the headings: 'AGREE', 'DISAGREE', 'I DON'T KNOW'.
4.   Pairs take turns in sticking their statement(s) in one of the three columns. Each pair explains the reasons for their choice, and the rest of the group can respond.

The statements may need to be read to younger children.

Cross-curricular links: Personal and Social Education (PSE).

Follow-up activities/extensions: read aloud the following story written by Maaike, a nine-year old girl, and ask the children to write down their answers to her questions before they discuss the story. The younger children can talk about it in a large circle.

BRAINS and MY THINKING

Look at that title. Have I got a brain? I don't think so, do you? Well, can you remember being a baby? I can't.

One day, I was sitting at a desk at school THINKING!! Look, at that word. Do you need a brain to think? That was the question I was thinking about. Well, I *think* that if we didn't have a brain, we would not be able to think. DO YOU THINK?!!

I asked if you can remember being a baby. Well, I can't. That day, I went to Kerry Kittman and asked 'Do you think you get a new brain from five years onwards?' She said: 'Don't know', and stormed off, leaving me standing helpless. So, now I turn to you and ask you the same question.

My answer is: 'Yes!', because I can't remember anything up to five years but I can from 5 years and over.

By Maaike. Age 9.

Photocopiable Sheet 3

THE THINKING GAME

---

1. My thoughts are not real, because I cannot see them, or touch them, or hear them.

---

2. When I am dreaming, it is like thinking, but then at night.

---

3. If I swap brains with my best friend, then I will have his thoughts, and he will have my thoughts.

---

4. I could not think, if I did not have eyes, ears, a nose, or touch.

---

5. When I am a grown-up, I will think in the same way as I do now.

---

6. I can only think my own thoughts, not somebody else's thoughts.

---

7. I am *always* thinking about something.

---

8. If I had different parents, I would think differently.

---

9. People who talk a lot, don't think a lot.

---

10. When I die, I stop thinking.

THOUGHTS AND FEELINGS

Aim: to think about the relationship between thoughts and feelings.

Objectives:
1.   Drawing abstract ideas.
2.   Distinguishing between thoughts and feelings.
3.   Completing a questionnaire.

Group size: minimum of eight; maximum of 35.

Timing: one hour.

Organization: normal classroom setting, but when discussing the exercise, use a circular setting.

Resources: pencils, rubber, colouring pencils/crayons; photocopies of the exercise.

What to do:
1.   First ask the children to make a drawing of:
     a) where they think their thoughts are;
     b) where they think their feelings are.
2.   Discuss the drawings in small groups and then as a whole class.
3.   Next, divide the class into pairs and give each pair a copy of Photocopiable Sheet 4: 'Thoughts and Feelings'. Read through the introduction and statements together as a class and then ask each pair to decide whether the 'feeling' words in each statement are feelings, or thoughts, or both. Call the children into a circle and discuss each statement together.

Cross-curricular links: Personal and Social Education (PSE).

Follow-up activities/extensions: discuss in small groups what life would be like without (1) thoughts, (2) feelings. Each group has to act out one situation they have been talking about in their small groups in front of the others.

Photocopiable Sheet 4

THOUGHTS AND FEELINGS

Often when we use the word *feel*, we mean different things. For example, we say 'I feel angry', or 'I feel scared' when we refer to an *emotion*. But we also say 'I feel pain', when we refer to a sore throat, and not to an emotion at all. Or, when we try to find our way to the toilet in the middle of the night we could say 'I feel my way to the light switch'. And we mean something else again when we say 'I feel certain that it will not rain today', which sometimes means that we just *hope* it will not rain, but at other times, we see it as an opinion based on reasons (e.g. the weather forecast). Some people believe that only in the latter case do our thoughts come in to it, but that in many cases feelings and thoughts are quite distinct. Have a look at the following examples, and see whether you find it easy to keep thoughts and feelings apart.

		Feeling	*Thought*	*Both*
1.	Christmas makes everyone *feel* very excited.	☐	☐	☐
2.	The dog next door has just died, and my neighbour *feels* very sad.	☐	☐	☐
3.	These football boots make my blisters *feel* worse.	☐	☐	☐
4.	I *feel* my Mum was wrong to send me to bed.	☐	☐	☐
5.	I *feel* anxious to figure out this maths problem.	☐	☐	☐
6.	Let me *feel* how warm the water is.	☐	☐	☐
7.	My brother *feels* unwanted.	☐	☐	☐
8.	These hamburgers make me *feel* really hungry.	☐	☐	☐
9.	I don't *feel* like a swim.	☐	☐	☐
10.	Some people *feel* very strongly about not eating meat.	☐	☐	☐

Chapter 9

A Communication Framework for English as an Additional Language (EAL) Learners

Jackie Holderness

Jackie Holderness has worked in primary schools in Britain and overseas. She has been a Senior Lecturer in Education at Oxford Brookes University for several years, specializing in the teaching of language and literature in the primary school. She has published several English coursebooks and books for teachers.

BACKGROUND

As a class teacher, I frequently encountered EAL children struggling to make sense of their surroundings and their lessons. Most of these children cope well, thanks to the care and intervention of their teachers and peers. A few, however, have to struggle in an unintentionally unsupportive and unstructured learning environment. The reason for this may be that, while all primary teachers have received training in the teaching of EAL, fewer are likely to have had practical experience of the problems facing a child learning at school in a language different from the language used at home. Teachers are anxious to provide the child with a systematic language programme, but are not always sure where to begin.

Teaching contexts vary greatly: there are classes where a certain mother tongue dominates, classes which contains a variety of languages; or classes where there are one or two children who use languages other than English at home and in their local community. EAL children also vary. They may have a good command of oral or written English; they may be able to speak well but not yet write fluently; they may be at a very elementary stage or even total beginners.

Some schools are virtually monolingual; however, even where a school does not yet need to offer provision for EAL learners, a whole-school policy is recommended. Multilingual schools will invariably have a policy but will probably wish to review, from time to time, certain aspects of the policy, e.g. initial assessment procedures, the involvement of bilingual support teachers, home-school links or approaches to biliteracy. All schools need to address how their children's awareness of Britain's linguistic diversity can be developed, enhanced perhaps within the broader context of study language projects.

With increasing job mobility and refugee movements in Europe, it can happen that a family suddenly arrives and needs both welcome and support. All schools would certainly be well advised to draw up a policy for newcomers and language support in general.

As with any kind of whole-school decision-making, the staff need to appreciate and sustain both the broad aims and the daily details of policy, so that the child perceives a consistent application of values and procedures.

The language support provided by specialist EAL teachers is usually invaluable. It often takes place in the classroom because separate provision or withdrawal for EAL children can be seen to be divisive or even racist. For much of their time, however, EAL children spend their time in the classroom, unsupported by specialist help, struggling to make sense of the work which they see going on and in which they desperately want to be involved. Yet the progress these children make is often remarkable because it is fuelled by their desire to belong. The playground is probably one of their most effective learning environments, but sustained progress is dependent on the class teacher's planning and strategies.

AIMS

This chapter will therefore attempt to consider the communicative needs, strategies and competences of children who are speakers of English as a second or other language (EAL). It hopes to offer teachers:

- a framework of communicative skills;

- a selection of communicative activities;

- guidance concerning assessment of children's communicative development.

STARTING OUT

Integrating and supporting

The first step to successful EAL teaching is to appreciate the nature and importance of the role of the class teacher. Our attitudes to the EAL child and our readiness to provide extra visual and linguistic support will serve as a model to the rest of the children.

The class teacher's role

As class teachers, we will aim to achieve the following:

INTEGRATE THE EAL CHILD

When a child first arrives, he/she may need a 'silent period'. The child listens and slowly comes to understand but may be shy of actually producing any language until several months have passed. This is not uncommon and teachers need to recognize it and be patient with the child.

With a new child, it is often helpful to choose two 'buddies', whose special task is to:

1. help the child find his/her way around the school;
2. teach the child English, by working alongside him/her.

I have found it best, if possible, to choose one child who is very capable and has a high *academic* status in the class, balanced by a child who may have his/her own language needs but enjoys a high *social* status in the class. This identifies the EAL child with high status groups and can lead to more general acceptance.

MODEL LEARNING STRATEGIES

If we can consciously demonstrate ways of memorizing, categorizing, comparing, checking and enquiring about language structures and vocabulary items, the EAL child will benefit enormously.

A general class discussion about how people learn a second language is invaluable, and can be very illuminating because it encourages children to reflect upon their own language skills and usage. The children in the class will soon emulate the helpful strategies demonstrated by their teachers:

*   simplification of vocabulary;
*   exaggeration of intonation and gesture;

- use of pictures, sketches or mime to clarify meaning;
- acceptance of incorrect phrases;
- provision of correct words as models;
- encouragement to repeat new words.

Whenever we see a child using an effective language teaching strategy with the EAL child, we should try to praise the child involved, thereby encouraging the others to use similar strategies.

SUPPORT UNDERSTANDING

Through simplified or appropriately paced intervention, teachers can check constantly to ensure as complete an understanding as possible for the EAL charges in our care. We need to provide realia and visual support during stories or whole-class sessions. It is important, obviously, to use voice, facial expression and mime, but most important are visual supports (e.g. cut-out pictures stuck on a flannelgraph), frieze or magnet-board, puppets, toys and real objects. It is essential to ensure the provision of picture dictionaries, tapes and other materials suited to the child's age and interests.

In short, EAL teaching aims to be:

- NEAR – learning needs to relate to the child's experience.
- DEAR – learning needs to affect the child and be meaningful.
- CLEAR – understanding is vital and instructions simple.

PREPARE FOR A NEW ARRIVAL

In order to prepare effectively for a newcomer it is essential to try and understand things from the child's point of view. On arrival, the EAL child will probably spend part of each day working individually, perhaps with the class teacher or with a support teacher. At the beginning, it is helpful to plan one main language activity per day to be performed with a partner. This can be complemented with a group task, a listening activity (e.g. a story) and some vocabulary building related to a topic. For much of the time, however, the child may have to work alone, learning as much English as possible in a short time. The child can achieve a great deal working alone, or in a pair, if provision is made in advance.

CASE STUDY 1: PREPARING A 'SURVIVAL PACK'

As class teacher, I was given a week's notice that a Russian child was due to join my class. I set about collecting a variety of resources to support his learning. These included:

1. A ring binder with loose pages for topic-based vocabulary, e.g. My Family/Food/School Words, an alphabetic collection of sheets to build up a dictionary, work-sheets, etc.
2. Several EFL materials, such as course books supported by activity books and cassettes. I gave the child the first level Pupil's Book and cassette, from which he learned a great deal by looking and listening. The activity books were useful to generate activities and work-sheet ideas.
3. A tape recorder, story books and cassettes.
4. Picture dictionaries. One should be arranged alphabetically with each entry illustrated. The second should be arranged in topics, e.g. 'At the Supermarket'.
5. A collection of 'visuals', taken from magazines and catalogues to teach and practise basic vocabulary.
6. Puppets, toys, games and language-free puzzles and number games.

Whenever the child was unable to cope with the main class activity, he was at least able to use the materials listed above to discover new words, usually working through them with another child. His parents were able to support some of his learning at home because I provided him with a selection of materials in addition to his regular reading books.

PLAN APPROPRIATELY FOR EACH CHILD

First we have to assess the child's linguistic competence. This can be carried out by making time for a one-to-one conference, which should include a discussion based around visual material (e.g. picture dictionary), a tour of the school, and observation of the child's interaction with peers. Observing the child in the class and playground will reveal his/her communicative needs. It is important to note observations, and the Jigsaw Assessment Sheet (page 178) may be a helpful starting-point. We need to plan for the child's development. Careful planning is essential for steady progress and effective integration.

MOVING ON

A communicative framework

The following six S's may be helpful when considering how to plan for EAL children: Self-esteem, Subjects, Strategies, Skills, Structures, Stories/Songs.

Self-esteem

At the centre of the language framework for the child should be the child herself. Because self-esteem is essential to learning, it needs to be the number one priority. Ensuring a warm welcome, demonstrating clear routines, giving the EAL child a special class responsibility and showing a genuine interest in the child's home, family and previous school will all help the child to feel valued in the class.

Subjects

The subjects or topics around which the EAL child's early vocabulary learning will centre are likely to be those which relate directly to:

1.   the child's experiences and world;

2.   the local and school environment;

3.   the class topics;

4.   the world of fantasy and imagination.

The figure below is a framework of suggested vocabulary areas, arranged in a language spiral (based on a similar spiral by John Kallie: 1992).

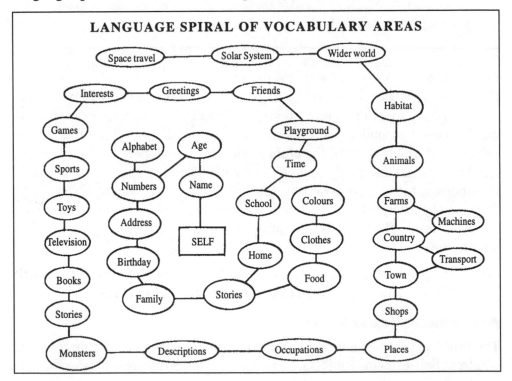

LANGUAGE SPIRAL OF VOCABULARY AREAS

CASE STUDY 2: A MINI BOOK

A 10-year-old child from Israel arrived in a monolingual and rural primary school. Her teacher made early contact with the parents and suggested that they provided the child with photographs of her home and life in Tel Aviv. These were used to initiate discussion, vocabulary teaching, and initial steps in writing English, with the teacher or another child labelling the pictures, with the child.

During the first few weeks in school, these photographs served as the main teaching focus as the child was encouraged to produce a series of mini books about herself. The approach helped to provide the child with a key to making friends. The other children began to bring in photos of their own and started to invite the Israeli child home to meet their families.

Strategies

Learning one's home language is usually an automatic, subconscious process, inextricably linked with establishing a place in one's family and culture. Learning a second language, however, can involve the child in more conscious reflection upon words, word order and differences between languages and cultures. The most successful language learners seem to be those who apply the following strategies.

- *Repetition* – echoing what is heard.
- *Memorization* – recalling by rote, e.g. days of the week.
- *Formulaic expression* – using phrases in context, e.g. 'Oh dear!'.
- *Verbal attention-getting* – e.g. 'Look at me . . .'
- *Answering in unison* – using other pupils as a cover for tentative speech.
- *Talking to self* – thinking aloud, possibly in a mixture of languages.
- *Anticipation* – thinking ahead, predicting meaning.
- *Monitoring* – self-correcting.
- *Appealing for assistance* – seeking support, e.g. 'So this means . . . ?'
- *Requesting clarification* – demanding extra information to make meaning clear.
- *Elaboration* – providing extra information to get meanings across

Usually these strategies are almost instinctive but children seem to benefit when they are made explicit, through demonstration or explanation.

Skills

Apart from the traditional language skills (L, S, R, W) there are other language skills which can contribute to the child's progress.

*   Body language, gesture and expression, so important to convey meaning.

*   Social ability to interact with others, building on what the previous speaker has said, turn-taking and co-operating on tasks, which involves sharing and negotiation.

*   Technical skills, such as writing English letters, handwriting, directionality in reading, dictionary and reference skills.

*   Cognitive skills which all children need to develop; the ability to compare and contrast, to categorize, to make hypotheses, to sequence, to interpret, synthesize and transfer skills from one context to another, e.g. science, art, P.E. activities.

Structures

The structures a child will need will reflect the purposes for which English is used. Some of the most useful initial structures have been identified below. The child needs to use English:

1. To establish relationships with others:

    Hello, I'm . . . I am   My name is . . .
    Let's . . .   Where do you live?
    You're . . .
    Do you . . . / Can you . . . / Will you . . . ?

2. To obtain information and respond appropriately:

    What's this . . . ?   It's . . .
    Where's . . .   It's on/under . . .
    Who's . . .   It's . . .
    When's . . .   Before, after . . .
    Why . . . ?   Because . . .
    Whose . . . ?   It's —'s . . .
    How many?   How much?

3. To convey information:

    First . . . next . . . then   My birthday is . . .
    It's + description/time   I come from . . .
    Bigger/biggest   This is . . .
    I live at . . .   I've got . . .
    My brother goes . . .   It's mine/yours/his

4. To reflect upon ideas, experiences and opinions:

    I don't know . . . /understand
    Maybe . . .
    What if . . . ?

5. To appreciate the feelings of others:

    Do you like . . . ?
    Are you . . . ?
    What do you want . . . ?

Stories

The use of story, rhyme, song and play should permeate all the other S's so far described. They ensure that language is presented and practised in context, and is repeated again and again and recycled in an enjoyable way, in a social setting. For these reasons they should form part of each and every day for the EAL child, even if it means simply steering the child towards a song or story tape to share with at least one friend. Sensitivity to diverse cultures is clearly important when choosing stories.

Repetitive stories with memorable phrases are obviously the most useful. Children will be familiar with story structures and conventions which will help them to predict meanings and follow the narrative. If we support stories with gesture and mime, visuals and real objects, we can ensure maximum involvement and understanding.

CASE STUDY 3: THE THREE LITTLE WOLVES . . .

A teacher read his class of 7-year-olds the story of *The Three Little Wolves and the Big Bad Pig* by Helen Oxenbury.

There were several children in the class who were learning English as a second or other language. The class was split into three groups and assigned a science investigation based upon house-building and the properties of different building materials.

The language focus for the EAL children was the use of the comparative and superlative, e.g. stronger than, the strongest, fastest, etc. The teacher drew these out during the feedback from each group and made labels to put on the wall in an area devoted to language.

Later, the EAL children were encouraged to act out the story while two other children read parts of it aloud. The short drama was presented to the class and the teacher then focused the EAL children upon the rolling rhythms of the text and the use of intonation, e.g.:

'The big, bad pig came prowling down the road . . . ' and 'He wasn't called big and bad for nothing . . . '

The final stage was to allow the EAL group to prepare a puppet play with their own retelling of the story.

Songs and games

Songs, rhymes and games are vitally important in helping EAL children enjoy learning English in memorable and social ways, e.g. 'There were ten in the bed', 'This is the house that Jack built', 'What's the time Mr Wolf?'

There are also many language games now available, including computer games. A useful criterion to consider is 'Will it encourage the EAL child to communicate with someone?' If the answer is yes, it may be helpful to pair up the EAL child with someone else who needs to be drawn out (e.g. an uncommunicative child). If the game is fun they will communicate without even realizing!

IN FULL SWING

Activities and organization

The activities included in this section are of more general application but could be easily adapted to suit particular topics. They are listed as examples of different groupings and organizational strategies.

Pairs

A short period of pair work each day is very important. The EAL child needs to operate in interaction with English-speaking classmates. Pairing the EAL child with different partners encourages the class to feel they are involved in the EAL child's progress. *Photocopiable Sheets 1, 2, and 3* are all useful for pair work.

ACTIVITY 1: INTERVIEWS

The EAL child and partner have to go around the class, or school, with a clipboard and instructions along the following lines:

Find someone who . . .

1. has black hair;
2. has blue eyes;
3. has a cat;
4. has a baby brother;
5. has a name beginning with S;
6. likes lemons;
7. lives in a flat;
8. can swim;
9. likes 'Home and Away';
10. can play the piano.

For numbers 1 to 5, the child will need to practise 'Do you have?' For the others, the questions are varied, 'Where do you live?', 'Do you like lemons?', 'Can you . . . ?'

The interview schedule can be adapted to practise a particular question form.

ACTIVITY 2: LISTEN AND DRAW

Each partner draws a picture, in secret. Then A describes it to B who must draw what is described without being able to see A's original. A can try to guide B during the process. Afterwards A shows B the original and they compare the picture. Next, B describes his drawing so that A can draw it.

This activity also works well, with each child making a secret shape from Unifix or Lego from exactly the same number and colours of pieces. Afterwards A describes his piece to B, so B can make it from a third set of pieces.

ACTIVITY 3: PACKING SUITCASES

The children each draw eight items of clothes on squares of card, but without showing each other their pictures. Each child puts her cards on a pile, face down. A starts by saying 'I'm going on holiday and I'm taking in my suitcase a . . . SHIRT.' A continues, turning up one card at a time until B says 'Stop!' If B has packed the same item he can interrupt. He looks through his pile, finds it and places it face up. He then continues in the same way, 'I'm going on holiday . . .' The first to finish wins. The children can then play Snap and use the cards as prompts for writing, dictionary work and so on.

ACTIVITY 4: MAPWORK

Give the children a large street map suitable for their age and ability level. A starts. 'I'm starting at the cinema/on the corner of James Street and Cowley Road . . . I turn left . . . I turn first right . . . I go past the park . . . I stop. Where am I?' B has to follow, but neither child may touch the map. They alternate turns and score one point each if the follower is correct.

Small groups

Group work means children working together towards a single goal (see Chapter 4 on SACLA). The composition of the group is important if the children are going to collaborate constructively. Size is also an important factor, with four being an optimum size to maximize involvement.

Group tasks across the curriculum can be augmented by the opportunity to play in the home or fantasy corner, to be involved in drama and role play, and to play games.

Group reading, where a group shares multiple copies of the same text, is very valuable, provided the book has strong visual support.

Many teachers worry that children of the same language communicate with each other without using and practising their English. However, children can be encouraged to use English to explain their work to other children in mixed language groups, or to an adult. Tasks can be set where English must be used, or times of the day designated when English only can be spoken. Meanwhile, the children can think and talk ideas through in their mother tongue and learn how to switch languages as appropriate.

ACTIVITY 5: GOING SHOPPING

The children sit in a small circle and take turns to build up the alphabetically-based shopping story.

Child 1: 'I'm going to the shops to buy an apple.'
Child 2: 'I'm going to the shops to buy an apple and some biscuits.'
Child 3: 'I'm going to the shops to buy an apple, biscuits and a cake.'

and so on.

If a mistake is made, the others say 'Oh no, you're not!' and the child is 'out'. (If the group has access to atlases, this game can be adapted to include capital or British cities – 'I'm going to Arundel, Bradford, Coventry . . . Amsterdam, Berlin, Cairo, etc.)

ACTIVITY 6: AUNT MARY'S CAT

This game follows similar alphabetical lines but focuses on adjectives.

Child 1 starts 'Aunt Mary's cat is an attractive cat.'
Child 2 'Aunt Mary's cat is a bad cat.'
Child 3 'Aunt Mary's cat is a cool cat.'

It is a good idea to get the children to write down the adjectives they choose for discussion later.

QUESTIONS AND ANSWERS

The pupils or you make question cards relating to the current class topic. For each question card there should be an answer card. The Q's and A's should be on different colour cards. Make a pile of each, shuffle them and give each child in the group one Q and one A card. Child 1 reads her Q aloud and then names someone. The child named looks at his answer card. If it's the correct answer to the Q he reads it aloud and the two cards are put in the centre as a pair. If not, he says 'Sorry I don't know.' He then asks his Q, naming a third child. They go on in this way around the circle until all the questions have been answered.

Whole class

When teaching the whole class, we need to maximize involvement for the EAL child. Whatever one feels about 'chalk and talk', the blackboard is a useful tool for explaining concepts we are teaching. By using diagrams, sketches, arrows and colours, we can make our teaching more visual. By writing key words and labels, we can ensure maximum linguistic support as well.

ACTIVITY 7: RESTAURANTS

Divide the class into two teams. Each child draws something he/she might be able to eat in a restaurant. Each team makes a pile at the front of each team's cards and shuffles them. Choose a waiter/waitress from each team. Child 1 in team A asks for a certain food. Waiter A turns up the top card, looks at it and says 'Yes, here you are', or 'No, I'm sorry. I haven't got any . . .' The card is left face up. Each customer ensures a new card is turned up. Any card which is face up can be served. Teams alternate turns and each time a new customer is chosen. Waiters can be changed every turn. The first team to 'consume' all its cards wins.

ACTIVITY 8: NUMBERS, TIMES AND DATES

Draw on the board two equal sets of numbers or times (2.45, etc.) or dates (June 13th). Divide the class into two teams. Call one person from each team to the board and give them a chalk. Choose a child to be 'caller'. The caller chooses one of the items and says it aloud. The first team member to circle the correct item wins a point for his/her team.

Becoming bilingual and biliterate

Once the EAL child can make herself understood in communicative situations, there is a danger that she stops moving towards increasing accuracy and a wider vocabulary. If a carefully planned approach is maintained, however, the child can hope to achieve successful bilingualism and biliteracy.

Linguists rarely agree about definitions of either of these terms. For the purpose of this chapter, we can consider a child is bilingual if he is a 'regular user of two languages' (Mayor, 1983). The bilingual child is able to select and use whichever language is appropriate to the task or audience. The EAL child's development in speaking and listening will be supported by her increasing awareness of the written form. Children whose first language uses a different alphabet and directionality (i.e. does not read left to right) will clearly need support in handwriting and the alphabet. It is important, however, that their knowledge of other scripts is valued and they should be given opportunity, where appropriate, to express their ideas in more than one script.

As with all writing activities, the tasks given need to have a clear purpose and audience for the child, who will certainly need to be given the chance to revise and redraft as necessary.

A sense of pride in being a writer in two or more languages should be fostered because, while true bilteracy is difficult to attain, the EAL child has, at least, the potential to achieve it.

CASE STUDY 4: TRANSLATIONS

A Hindi child who had been studying English at school for four years was encouraged to write about the two places she associated with the word 'Home', while working on a class topic about houses and homes. The teacher suggested that the child should enlist the knowledge and support of her family and write about her home village in India in Bengali. She wrote about her home town in the Midlands in English, creating her own dual language text. Later, with the help of a bilingual support teacher and a group of Bengali speakers, she provided translations for both sections of her book. The result was something she was very proud of, and her role as 'translator' firmly established. Thereafter, she was often asked to label things in Hindi or simply to teach someone the Hindi word for something. Another child produced a translation of a story in French, which his mother had worked on at home.

Monitoring progress

Monitoring the EAL child's development is clearly important. It may be helpful to use a framework of identifiable communicative skills so that there is a record of the child's progress over time. The first assessment sheet (Photocopiable Sheet 4A) is designed as an initial assessment form on entry to a school. The second assessment sheet (4B) is designed to help the school to begin to chart the child's language progress in English and to record a child's achievements. Other goals or achievements can be added as appropriate in the blank spaces. Hopefully, most EAL children would develop the majority of these skills over a one-year period.

KEY POINTS

Try to vary groupings and contexts for interaction.

Ensure learning is Near, Dear and Clear to the child.

Six S's: self-esteem, strategies, skills, subjects, structures, stories . . .

Offer support and maximize understanding for child, using visuals and key words.

Linguistic and cognitive achievements in the first language need to be valued.

(TESOL: Teaching English to Speakers of Other Languages)

Teachers' Notes 1

CLASSROOM VOCABULARY INFORMATION GAP

Aim:
1.   To teach or revise classroom vocabulary.

Objectives:
1.   Working in a range of situations.
2.   Developing their ability to ask questions.
3.   Giving and understanding instructions.
4.   Having opportunities to reflect on their effectiveness in speaking.

Group size: pairs.

Timing: 1 hour 20 minutes (4 × 20-minute sessions) – 1) a, 2) b, 3) c, 4) d.

Resources: one pair of scissors per pupil, glue, two copies of the lower part of Photocopiable Sheet 1 (grids).

Organization:
1.   The children cut out the pictures to make small cards. Each partner uses the cards and the real objects to check/teach the words.
2.   The children use the cards to play Pelmanism (the memory game) or Snap.
3.   They stick their pictures on the lower part of the sheet without showing each other either arrangement, which they will try to guess.
4.   They then use the grids and ask each other questions.

What to do:
Each pupil, having stuck the pictures in an arrangement of their choice, keeps the sheet hidden. One pupil (A) then takes his blank grid sheet and asks the other pupil (B) questions to try and establish B's arrangement. 'Where's your paint? Is it on the top? Is it next to the bin?' etc. B may not show or point to his grid. A should write or sketch the objects in pencil on his blank grid sheet and when he thinks they are all correct, should compare his sheet with B's. One point is scored for each correct placement.

Next A takes out her arrangement and keeps it hidden. B takes his blank sheet and asks A similar questions. The pupil at the end with the most correct replica of his partner's arrangement wins.

Cross-curricular links: Maths, e.g.:
1.   Make a map of the classroom.
2.   Make a model classroom.
3.   Weigh the objects.
4.   Make a matrix and identify which materials each object is made from.

Follow-up activities/extensions:
1.   Once the children are familiar with the game, it can be used to practise vocabulary from any topic.
2.   The pupils could make up a board game about the classroom.

CLASSROOM VOCABULARY INFORMATION GAP

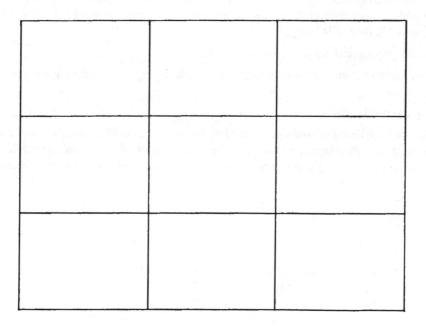

TOPIC BINGO

Aims:
1.   To introduce or revise vocabulary (food, transport, clothes, household objects).
2.   To categorize words into topic families.

Objective: extending children's vocabulary; describing objects.

Group size: pairs.

Timing: 2 × 30-minute sessions.

Resources: scissors (1 per pair of children); Photocopiable Sheet 2; an envelope per child (used); small pieces of paper; one A4 grid with 24 squares per child.

Organization: the cards have to be cut out and each topic family can be put into a recycled envelope, labelled with the topic and the child's name. The names of each item can be written on small pieces of paper for matching words and pictures later on.

Use the pictures and other visuals to teach the words. With beginners, teach one or two topics at a time. Children at an intermediate level should be able to handle all four topics.

What to do: the children should cut out the pictures and spread them face upwards on the desk. One by one, they describe a picture but avoid saying the name of the object.

Give each child a grid of six squares per topic. The children can label each grid with the topic words (transport, household, clothes, food).

They should then choose three cards to put in an envelope, out of the way.

Start to play Bingo, calling the name of each item and letting the children put the pictures into their grids. Switch from topic to topic, calling the items at random until a child has one complete grid. He then calls 'Bingo!'

Carry on playing until all four grids are called.

Let the children then play other games with the cards, e.g. the memory game (Pelmanism pairs) or Snap.

Cross-curricular links: Topic work.

Follow-up activities/extensions: the children collect other small pictures and make up topic dictionaries for other topics, e.g. animals, plants, toys, sports, insects, birds; the children play I-Spy in pairs using a topic-based picture dictionary, either their own or a commercially produced one.

TOPIC BINGO

Teachers' Notes 3

PREPOSITIONS MATCHING GAME

Aims:
1. To introduce/revise prepostitions.
2. To encourage reading of simple sentences.

Objectives:
1. Developing confidence, precision and competence in reasoning.
2. Having opportunities to reflect on their effectiveness in speaking, learn about variation in vocabulary.

Group size: pairs or threes.

Timing: 2 × 30-minute sessions 1) a, b, c; 2) d.

Organization:
1. The children cut out the pictures and sentences.
2. The EAL child is taught prepositions of place using the picture cards.
3. The sentences are read and matched to the pictures.
4. The children play the matching game.

Resources: scissors, Photocopiable Sheet 3.

What to do: each child spreads out the picture cards in front of him, face up. Both children's sentences are put in a big pile, face down. The children take it in turns to turn up a sentence card and then match it to one of their own pictures. If they already have covered a picture, the sentence card is returned to the bottom of the pile. Each sentence should be read aloud, with the EAL child being helped as necessary.

Cross-curricular links:
1. Recycle prepositions in PE or movement lessons, perhaps playing 'Simon Says', e.g. 'Stand behind B'. Simon says 'B stand next to A'. 'A and B lie under a skipping rope', etc.

Follow-up activities/extensions:
1. Help children to read *Rosie's Walk* by Pat Hutchins, and act out or prepare an OHP story about an animal's journey, which includes as many of these prepositions as possible. They can draw pictures on an OHP acetate and uncover each picture as they tell their story.
2. Using toys, child A instructs child B to move a toy around, 'Put the bear inside the boat, under a book, etc . . .' Take turns.
3. Make a wall display or booklet with illustrations of other locational prepositions e.g. through, beside etc.

PREPOSITIONS MATCHING GAME

The cat is on the chair		The boy is above the girl	
The cat is under the chair		The boy is below the girl	
He's running across the road		The dinosaur is outside	
She's in front of the elephant		The tree is near the house	
She's behind the elephant		The tree is next to the house	
He's in the boat		He's running beside the road	
He's out of the boat		The balloon is going up	
The dinosaur is inside		The parachute is coming down	

Teachers' Notes 4A & B

ASSESSMENT RECORDS

Aims:
1.   To assess initial competence in English and other languages.
2.   To record children's progress over time.

Objectives:
1.   Enhancing teacher's awareness of child's language capabilities and needs so as to inform future planning.
2.   Involving older children in their own assessment.

Group size: individual.

Timing: the initial interview, preferably with parents or guardians and, if necessary, translators present, should take from 30 to 60 minutes. The progress record is a continuous document, which can be filled in steadily over the first year in school.

What to do:
1.   Try to complete as much of the information on Photocopiable Sheet 4A as possible and copy it for any member of staff who will be working with the child. Use the backs of the sheets to record your early observations of the child in school.
2.   Complete Photocopiable Sheet 4B as and when possible and use it to structure teaching sessions. When the child has been observed demonstrating a particular language competence, colour in the relevant piece of jigsaw. Older children should be encouraged to colour in their own pieces, with help.

Follow-up activities/extensions: introduce an 'I can . . .' tree or noticeboard where all children can have celebrated some achievement or recently mastered skill. The EAL child's progress can then become something the whole class is involved in.

INITIAL ASSESSMENT FORM

Name:	Pronounced:		
Family position: e.g. GG*B*B	Age: Religion:		
Languages spoken at home:	Mother:	Father:	Other:
Languages child can understand:			
Languages child can speak:			
Languages child can read:			
Languages child can write:			
Language tuition received outside school:			
Attitude to school:	Week 1	Week 2	Week 3
Communicative confidence Adults Children			
Body language:			

Photocopiable Sheet 4B

PROGRESS RECORD

Chapter 10

Using News Events for Media-based Discussions

Jim Honeybone

Jim Honeybone taught English, for many years, in a large community college. He has always been keen to encourage genuine debate and independence of thought, reasoning and opinion among his pupils. He is currently exploring the role of news-based discussion in EFL in the Republic of China and has found that his approaches work with all age ranges and cultures.

BACKGROUND

The news is full of controversy. The papers are full of debate. If we are to help prepare children to be effective citizens of the future then the classroom should be a place of debate and controversy as well.

Through the media, children and their parents are kept in touch with world events. The children will probably know something about the news item chosen for discussion but their prior level of knowledge is unimportant. The children's contributions need to be valued, as long as they are thoughtfully reasoned opinions.

About ten years ago, therefore, I started the publication of a news-sheet, called *CH* (Contemporary History) *Weekly,* which is a topical news prompt for use in the classroom to stimulate media-based discussion. *CH Weekly* is an A4 page with factual information about a current controversial issue with questions for discussion. From using spirit masters in the early days, the publication is now produced using laser technology. There is a team of teachers who take turns to write the weekly news-sheet, and *CH Weekly* has been made available to schools up and down the country.

With or without the support of the news-sheet, this chapter aims to provide an approach to the study of current issues which develops skills of oracy and debate among older primary and secondary pupils. However, the approach could be adapted to suit younger children. The approach is based upon a deliberate move from informal, small-group discussion to a larger discussion forum. This development has a role to play in any primary classroom. Likewise, the guidelines for organizing such discussions could be helpful in a variety of teaching contexts.

AIMS

This chapter aims to describe a particular approach to the study of news events with pupils aged 8 to 16, as described in the previous paragraph. It uses events and opinions presented through the media, e.g. daily newspapers. Using the media ensures:

- the topic is always fresh;

- the issues chosen are likely to relate to the children's experience;

- access to the controversies humans face.

It is important that controversy in the classroom need not involve the teacher. The debate should be among the children, uninhibited by the teacher's opinion. Children show enormous enthusiasm for discussing topical issues with minimal teacher input. Media-based discussions therefore aim to:

- make children think deeply about the reporting of world events;

- make children discuss increasingly complex issues;

- enable children to differentiate clearly between fact, opinion and prejudice, assess and interpret arguments and opinions with increasing precision and discrimination;

- encourage children to present factual information in a clear and logically structured manner in a widening range of situations;

- help them to understand the importance of reasoning to support an opinion;

- express and justify individual feelings, opinions and viewpoints with increasing sophistication;

- discuss issues in both small and large groups, taking account of the views of others;

- encourage children to develop debating skills and confidence;

- demonstrate that committee work and discussion can be enjoyable;

- communicate with other groups in a wide range of situations, e.g. collaborating on an assignment where a specific outcome is required;

- use their reading of news articles to discuss and experiment with different written genres and their relationship to audience and purpose . . .

STARTING OUT

1. Planning

Planning the lesson involves several stages. You will need to:

- choose the topic;
- write out the facts;
- decide upon the opinion questions;
- possibly plan a follow-up activity, e.g. writing, study of reports or a formal debate.

These stages have been outlined in further detail below.

a) *Choosing the topic*
The choice of topic will depend upon the age and interests of the class and the current news items. It is helpful to warm up the proceedings with a quick, factual question-and-answer session, connected with the topic. There is no argument at this stage but the children are encouraged to start thinking about the topic.

b) *Writing out the facts*
Ten or twelve factual statements about a news event are written down, without comment (see page 189). When writing out the facts, it is most helpful if the facts cover both sides of a case with equal objectivity, but it is not essential. The key to a successful discussion will always be the quality of the opinion questions which are asked.

c) Deciding the opinion questions

Questions which will provoke as wide a range of response as possible are thought out. The aim is to get the children to argue among themselves. A question which receives unanimous agreement is not a successful one. The point of the questions is to stimulate thought, reasoning and controversy, by getting children to decide what their own opinion is on a matter and then explain why they hold that opinion.

d) Planning a follow-up activity

It is not, of course, necessary to plan any follow-up to the discussion. The small and large group discussions about the media and its representation of the chosen topic are the main reasons for the news session. There are, however, a variety of follow-up activities which may be helpful to extend the children's understanding of the media and current affairs.

2. Writing

The discussion can be followed by a 'newspaper' writing session. An outline or grid can be useful *(Photocopiable Sheet 2)*. The children can invent their own newspaper titles. These are frequently based on their surnames, e.g. *Wayne's Weekly.*

The children may also devise a headline for an article about the topic just discussed. The 'facts' section is drawn very small so the children have to be selective. Children with writing difficulties can be supported by the teacher scribing a few facts which the child can then copy down.

The opinion is the most important section and should be written as a straight 'leading article' of the kind found in newspapers. Once again, though, opinions need to be supported by reasons. The length of the article will be dependent on time and ability. Children who enjoy writing can use the reverse side of the sheet. There is also a cartoon section. Reluctant artists can use matchstick people and speech bubbles.

3. Media study

Another interesting way to follow up the discussion is to let the class examine different reports about the same event, clipped from that week's newspapers or even recorded from the radio and television.

4. Debates

In class, three or four speakers are elected to represent the two sides, for and against the motion, e.g. 'The class thinks that cycle helmets are a waste of money.'

MOVING ON

A familiar routine helps the children feel secure and enables both you and the class to use a limited time period economically. A typical NEWS lesson might therefore follow this format.

Starters

A typical news session starts with the whole class thinking about the topic prompted by questions, from the teacher.

The facts

A volunteer then reads aloud the facts, but a second volunteer is then asked to rephrase the fact in his or her own words. Vocabulary is thus extended because in every lesson of this type, new words are being encountered and alternatives explored.

It is important to distinguish fact from opinion. One important point in connection with the difference between fact and opinion is that children accept, almost intuitively, that a person's opinion can also be a fact. It's a fact that the leader of the opposition said 'I think the government is wrong.' The fact is that the leader of the opposition holds that opinion. In the follow-up written work, facts can be very clearly divided from opinions so that any ambiguity is quickly resolved.

Opinion questions

The opinion questions are read out one at a time, and checks made to ensure their meaning is clear.

Small group work

The class then splits up into small groups. Groups of four are chosen at random and consist of two girls and two boys. Because everyone is in a randomly chosen group, they quickly overcome their initial disappointment over not being with their friends. Any twos or threes which result are prioritized as fours next time. The groups are changed every four weeks, so that each member of the group has a chance to be group reporter.

Through this group work, everyone can present their views and listen to each other in an informal situation.

The groups know that they have five minutes to sort out their opinions and their justifications for those opinions. As teacher, you can walk around, checking on the group interaction and progress, and finding out which questions are generating the most discussion or enthusiasm.

Each group has a group reporter who records the discussion using a clipboard. The children who find writing difficult can be encouraged to use their own shorthand.

```
        X              X              X              X
    X + X          X + X          X + X          X + X
        X              X              X              X
```

Whole-class discussion

The whole-class discussion takes place next, with the children seated in a forum or horseshoe shape. It is essential to ensure that everyone can see the face of each speaker.

a) The pupil secretary

Within the class discussion, one child is appointed or volunteers to hold a position of special responsibility, called the pupil secretary, which is crucial to the effective organization of the discussion. The secretary(s) should sit next to the teacher who acts as a neutral chairperson. The class should sit in a circle or a horseshoe so that everyone can maintain eye contact.

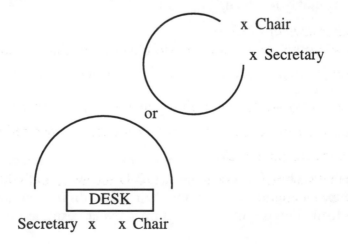

The children very much enjoy being secretary. It is therefore a good idea to organize a weekly rota so that everyone gets a chance. The secretary, armed with a clipboard and pen, sits next to the teacher. The secretary's task is to note down the names of all the children who put their hands up as nearly as possible in the order their hands are raised. As the discussion proceeds, the secretary then calls out the name of the next in line to contribute.

At the start of the discussion, ask the secretary who is first, the name is called and discussion begins. No hands are left waving in the air. If someone has forgotten the point they wished to make or no longer wish to contribute, they can say 'Pass' or that they agree with an earlier speaker. They may also ask to be moved to the bottom of the list. A particularly controversial opinion will not create a rabble of noise, but a forest of hands and a very busy secretary.

The pupil secretary appears to solve the problem often posed by class discussion, that of class control. What is lost in spontaneity, through a strict regard for the order of speaking, is far outweighed by the atmosphere of concentration and anticipation which is engendered.

Quieter children are greatly encouraged by the secretary system. They think out their point, get on the list and then have an opportunity to say their views in an ordered situation, without fear of an impulsive response of any kind.

The teacher can encourage the very shy to join the list, if they seem to be reluctant to participate at all. The teacher can also ask the secretary to give priority to those children who have not yet spoken, if time is running short or certain children are tending to dominate the list. The discussion usually lasts for at least twenty minutes but not all questions may be discussed.

At the end of the discussion, the secretary has a list of all the children who have contributed, which can be useful for assessment purposes.

b) The teacher as neutral chair

During the whole-class discussion, the teacher acts as chairperson and has six major functions:

1. To keep control – refusing to allow anyone to speak out of turn.

2. To keep a constant check that each contribution is supported by a reason.

3. To ensure each point is clear.

4. To correct statements which are factually incorrect, but without giving his/her own opinion.

5. To decide how long is spent on each opinion question. It is a good idea to ask the secretary to draw a line under the last name for a particular question. When the secretary announces 'the line', the decision to move to another question can always be reviewed.

6. As teacher, you should take no part in the discussion. This has three objectives:

    First, you are released to concentrate on an overview of the discussion.

    Second, the class perceives that it is their discussion, that their opinions are valid and will not be supported or refuted by the teacher. Children very quickly appreciate the fact that there is no teacher contribution to their discussion. Children may ask you what you think about a topic. The best reply is 'I can give you my opinion after the discussion.' If they do ask you later, in private, you can then tell them what you think and why.

    Finally, being neutral enables the teacher to observe the children more closely for assessment purposes, noting down comments which seem significant.

IN FULL SWING

Since the approach provides well-defined roles for children to manage themselves effectively, you are freed to listen, observe and gather evidence of individual oracy needs and achievements.

It is useful to have a clipboard with a sheet with the statements of attainment for the NC Speaking and Listening, together with a list of names, because you can tick those areas where a child seems to be confident or needing some support or practice.

At the end of the term, it is valuable to encourage the children to look back over the topics discussed and reflect upon those which generated the most debate or controversy. It is also important to allow them to evaluate their own progress and consider their personal debating achievements. They can think about the skills they have developed and those which still need further work, e.g. building upon previous speakers' contributions or voice projection.

As the year progresses, the children often express a desire to choose their own news item. They can then, in groups, produce their own facts and opinion questions. Eventually, children can take on the role of the neutral chair, taking turns week by week. At first, it may be helpful to split the class into smaller groups of about ten children, each with a secretary. You can then move between the three groups, offering advice. Eventually, the children's sense of independence and ownership of the discussion increases. The children become more confident when expressing their opinions, tolerant of the opinions of others and enthusiastic about current affairs.

KEY POINTS

Make sure that you choose news items that are likely to provoke debate and relate to the interests of the class.

Encourage children to support their opinions with reasons.

Discussions with the whole class rely on careful seating arrangements.

Insist that the chairperson remains very strictly neutral.

Agree procedures for each kind of discussion and ensure that the pupil secretary and the chairperson are strict about following these procedures.

Teachers' Notes 1

POCKET MONEY

Aim: to discuss a news item, e.g. newspaper article on pocket money.

Objectives:
1. Using Contemporary History approach for whole-class discussion.
2. Distinguishing facts from opinions.

Group size: whole class/small groups.

Timing: any time between 30 minutes and an hour or even longer.

Organization: whole class. Hand out sheets; volunteers read aloud the facts and the opinion questions. Split class into small groups. Allow five minutes to generate opinion questions (see p. 182).

Resources: one copy of Photocopiable Sheet 1 ('Pocket Money') per child.

What to do: discuss questions in small groups, encouraging children to express their opinions on the topic and to explain the reasons for those opinions. The group reporter records the discussion. The small groups join together for the whole-class discussion in which one pupil acts as 'pupil' secretary. Draw together for whole-class discussion.

Cross-curricular links: English, history, humanities, PSE, economics.

Follow-up activities /extensions:
1. Newspaper writing.
2. Children write their own information sheet.
3. Children chair their own class discussion.
4. Debates and assemblies.

Photocopiable Sheet 1

POCKET MONEY

Starters	1. What do you think is the average weekly pocket money for this class? 2. What is it that pocket money is most likely to be spent on? 3. If any is saved, what is it likely to be saved for?
News	Pocket money: 'North gets nearly twice as much as South-East.'
Facts	1. The Halifax Building Society does an annual survey of its young savers. 2. The questions include – (a) How much pocket money do you get a week? (b) Do you earn it by doing jobs around the house? (c) Do you save it or spend it? (d) If you save it – what for? If you spend it – what on? 3. The results show that the average weekly pocket money for under-11s in the UK is £1.40; up from £1.10 last year. 4. Children in the North of England get the most – £1.80; children in the South-East get the lowest – £1.00. 5. 51% of children have to do jobs either for all or part of their pocket money. 6. Jobs include washing/drying pots (34%); general tidying up (23%); tidying own bedroom/make own bed (21%); hoovering (11%); gardening/washing the car (7%). 7. Most pocket money is spent on sweets, then holidays/trips, then toys, then books/magazines/comics, and last, gifts. 8. 48% save more than they spend; 23% save it all; 18% spend more than they save and 9% spend it all. 9. Most saving is for holidays; next for large/expensive toys; next for gifts; next for computer equipment/software/bike, and last for the future/sports equipment.
Opinion	1. Does anything in the survey surprise you? Explain your answer. 2. What, in your opinion, should the average amount of pocket money be for your age group? Give your reason. 3. Should all your pocket money be a right or should it be earned? Why? 4. In your opinion, which jobs have parents got a right to expect children to do at home? Give your reasons. 5. In your opinion, what percentage of pocket money should be saved and what percentage spent? Explain why. 6. What, in your opinion, are the most worthwhile things to spend pocket money on? Your reasoning?
Cartoon	Lots of matchstick children if you find sketching tricky . . .
Map	The 'Halifax' did a regional breakdown of their results. On a map of the British Isles shade in different colours where you think the following regions are: Scotland, Northern Ireland, North, North-West, Midlands, East, South-East, South Wales and West, London.

Teachers' Notes 2

THE *CH* NEWSPAPER

Aims:
1. To encourage awareness of newspaper genre format.
2. To follow up class discussion with a writing activity.

Objectives:
1. Organizing and structuring writing in a variety of ways.
2. Distinguishing degrees of formality for unfamiliar audiences.

Group size: individuals, pairs or small groups.

Timing: 30 to 40 minutes for Year 5, 6 and 7 classes.

Organization: prepare outlines or grids. Encourage children to choose their own newspaper titles and to devise a headline for an article about the topic discussed.

Resources: A4 paper and the discussion sheet about the chosen topic (e.g. pocket money).

What to do: explain the format of Photocopiable Sheet 2 to the children. Ensure everyone is clear about the need for conciseness of language. Encourage children to rehearse their idea through talk. The children then select the facts for the facts section. They should then plan, draft and redraft their opinion section. Display the finished newspaper articles where they can be read during the following week.

Cross-curricular links: English, history, humanities, PSE, economics.

Follow-up activities /extensions:
1. Mark the places that were in the week's news on blank maps.
2. Calculate approximate percentages of good news, bad news and advertising.

Wall display: the classroom wall display of newspapers attracts a lot of close attention and controversy and can be regularly and easily up-dated. Ask the children to choose their two best newspapers from the half term and display them as 'Views on the News'.

THE *CH* NEWSPAPER

Use this sheet to draw up the frontpage of your newspaper on a blank sheet of A4 paper. The measurements are an indication of how much space you should allocate to each section.

Title	
Headline	10 cm
Reporter (byline):	
Facts (11 cm)	Opinion
Cartoon (8 cm)	

Teachers' Notes 3

EXTRA! EXTRA!

Aims:
1. To encourage children to discuss newspapers.
2. To heighten children's awareness of different newspaper departments, roles and types of articles.
3. To help children find their way around within a newspaper.

Objectives:
1. Reading and talking about texts with a variety of structural and organizational features.
2. Reading and discussing a range of non-fiction.
3. Identifying and commenting on key features . . . in a variety of media.

Group size: groups of three or four.

Timing: 30 minutes to 1 hour.

Organization: collect together a wide variety of newspapers. Divide the class into groups of three or four and give each group a selection of papers and a large sheet of blank paper and glue.

Resources: a large sheet of paper, three or four old newspapers, felt pens, three or four pairs of scissors and glue for each group of children.

What to do: read through Photocopiable Sheet 3 and discuss the different types of newspaper features. Explain that each group is going to find different types of articles and present them, labelled, on the large sheet. They can then compare sheets with another group, looking for similarities and differences. Articles will be taken from several papers.

Cross-curricular links: maths, science (weather), art, history (current affairs), PE.

Follow-up activities/extensions: produce a class newspaper, assigning roles and writing articles relating to the school; write letters to the editors of national newspapers, outlining their papers' successes and areas for improvement.

EXTRA! EXTRA! FIND OUT ALL ABOUT IT!

Types of article

- **Editorial:** The Editor chooses the 'COPY' for the paper and writes the Editorial, which is the newspaper's official opinion on events.

- **News stories:** These can be local, national or international. They provide information and should be based on fact.

- **Letters:** Readers write to the Editor, offering their opinions.

- **Features:** These often complement news stories and provide background information. They cover subjects like fashion, cookery, cars, books, gardens, travel, science and education.

- **Sport:** Articles are supplemented by notification of matches, results, league tables and comment.

- **Cartoons and comic strips:** Sometimes topical. Designed to amuse.

- **Advertisements:** Most newspapers earn a lot of money from adverts.

- **Weather and other services, such as exchange rates.**

To do: in groups of three or four, find and cut out one example of each type of article. Stick them on a large sheet of paper. Label each one. Compare and discuss your examples with other groups.

Now see if you can find the following:

- The newspaper's address.
- The circulation or distribution figure.
- The newspaper's number.
- The late news/Stop Press column.
- The newspaper's telephone number and fax number.

Teachers' Notes 4

DEBATE SCRIPT

Aims:
1. To encourage children to take the role of chair during a class discussion.
2. To introduce the class to the format for debate.

Objectives:
1. Communicating to different audiences.
2. Reflecting on how speakers adapt their vocabulary, tone, pace and style.

Group size: whole class.

Timing: 30 minutes.

Organization:
1. Decide upon a motion, e.g. the class thinks that the school's uniform should be abolished.
2. Elect three or four speakers to represent the two sides, for and against the motion.

Resources: one script sheet for the chairperson.

What to do: read through the script with the whole class and then with the first child to chair the debate. In further debates, encourage the previous chairperson to read the script through with his/her successor. Allow the child some time to write notes on the script sheet, including names, etc. The child should be able to refer to the script during the debate.

Cross-curricular links: dependent on the subject of the debate.

Follow-up activities/extensions: get the children in groups to write down some of the phrases which were used by the chairperson. Which group has remembered the most?

DEBATE SCRIPT

This is a model script for chairing a debate. Read it through before you chair the debate or refer to it as necessary.

PUPIL CHAIR: ORDER! ORDER! Welcome to the Debate.

The motion before the class is:_____

Speaking for the motion is: _____

Speaking against the motion is: _____

Your secretary is: _____

I call on _____to propose the motion.

Thank you. I call on _____to oppose the motion.

Thank you. I call on _____ to speak second for the motion.

Thank you. I call on _____to speak second against the motion, etc. for however many platform speakers there are.

You may now have a two-minute break to digest and discuss what you have just heard and may prepare your contribution to the debate.

ORDER! ORDER! (Wait for total silence) The motion is now open to the floor _____ (as many speakers making points, not asking questions, as can be taken in the time allotted).

Thank you the floor. It is now time to sum up.

I call on _____to sum up the case *against* the motion. Thank you.

I call on _____to sum up the case *for* the motion. Thank you.

We will now vote. The motion before the class is

_____

Those in favour _____ Those against _____ Those abstaining _____
(Secretary notes figures).

The vote was as follows. For _____ Against _____ Abstentions _____

I therefore declare the motion carried/defeated (won/lost).

Thank you for attending the debate. I declare the debate closed.

Chapter 11

Oracy and Children with Special Educational Needs

Gordon Baddeley

The author was a Professional Officer with the National Oracy Project and has written widely on speaking and listening in educational contexts, including teaching Talking and Learning at Key Stage 2 (1991). Many thanks are due to the teachers in the National Oracy Project Development Phase 1988–91, from whose work the Case Studies are drawn.

BACKGROUND

There is for all of us a gap between that which we know, understand, or can do, and the extent to which we can communicate these things to others. Teaching and learning is largely about reducing that gap.

The Education Act 1981 states that 'a child has "special educational needs" if he has a learning difficulty which calls for special educational provision to be made for him'. Eighteen per cent of the school population are deemed to fall into this definition during their school career, and are taught in mainstream schools.

The National Oracy Project was a six-year curriculum development programme concerned with the relationships between talk and learning. Teachers within the Project used the opportunity to develop strategies to help children who had specific learning needs. Such children seemed to fall into two broad categories:

- the children who struggled to learn and:
  - who needed help and time in approaching understanding;
  - who had an obvious physical or sensory disability;
  - who had difficulty in relating to others and could become either isolated from the learning, or disruptive of the learning of other children;
- children who learned quickly:
  - who picked up and remembered things much more quickly than others;
  - who were afraid that their giftedness might identify them as different from their peers;
  - who were not stretched or challenged by the quality of interaction with their teacher or peers.

Such judgements about children are of course always relative, and are often, at least initially, difficult to substantiate through objective testing. Teachers followed their own instincts where they felt that there was a reason for concern, and began their observations from there.

AIMS

This chapter draws upon the principles and strategies which class teachers of children with special needs have found particularly useful in planning to enhance the role of talk in the learning process.

STARTING OUT

Looking at context

In the first instance, teachers began to think about what was meant by special educational needs in relation to oracy. They identified two areas of concern.

1. There are those who have problems with oracy itself. Reluctance to speak, or a physical disability in speech, can hinder participation in learning for both able and less able pupils. These problems may be physiological or emotional; they may relate to experiences outside the school; they may be part of a growing sense of failure within school. The National Curriculum insists that 'all pupils share the right to a broad and

balanced curriculum, including the National Curriculum' (1989). The issue is not one of 'This child cannot participate, and therefore I must find alternatives'; it is more to do with 'This child has a right to participate, and therefore I must find ways to make it possible.'

2.   There are those who are more articulate than they appear to be, who need to utilize their strengths in oracy to overcome, or compensate for, or simply make more explicit, difficulties and competences in learning. 'Pupils with specific learning difficulties will benefit from teaching approaches which make best use of their oral strengths and avoid their difficulties with written communication . . .' ('A Curriculum for All', NCC 1989).

CASE STUDY 1: STORY-MAKING

One group of teachers in the same school listened to and read together a record of a group of children making up a story. One of the children in the group had been identified by the school as having learning difficulties, but the transcript did not name the children. The transcript proved to be a means of getting a new insight into what this child could do, since he seemed to be participating and contributing well to the work of the group. The teachers realized that special needs for many children related to the demands within a given context, since as part of a group story-making activity this child participated fully and usefully.

Children may give an impression of lack of competence because they are unable, or unwilling, to express what they know. Often the accepted channel for the communication of competence, let us say writing, is the very area in which a child has difficulty. In such cases their attempt to express what they know through writing may be demonstrating a lack of competence, not in their knowledge and understanding, but in their written expression of it.

Giving status to oracy as a way of approaching and presenting learning gives to all children, including those who have particular difficulties with reading and writing, a means of letting others know more fully the levels of their understanding and competence. Teachers therefore set themselves to listen carefully as children talked. When teachers made time to watch, listen, make notes, or to talk more with individual or pairs of pupils, they obtained much more information upon which to base decisions about provision for children's learning. They were also able to monitor the degree to which pupils accepted and built on the contributions of others, giving time and taking turns. Listening also clarified when, and for what purpose, teachers intervened in group discussions.

CASE STUDY 2: MONITORING TALK

One teacher of Year 4 children made a systematic enquiry into her own use of talk. She set herself guidelines:

- take the direction from the child; comment on and extend only what the child says;
- wait for children to think about what they wish to say;
- add personal information of my own;
- allow the interaction of children together without feeling a need to comment or make a judgement;
- demonstrate by my attention and demeanour that children's talk is important to me.

The teacher monitored her conversations with children by recording them onto tape from time to time, and listening to the tape later. She also kept notes in which she reflected on her use of talk in various classroom situations (whole-class, one-to-one, small group, giving information or instructions, etc.). It was hard work, but 'it gave me a deeper understanding of how I influenced talk in the classroom, and helped me to work more closely within the guidelines I had set for myself. Children talked more about what was important to them, or used me to work out an idea, so that I became more aware of the needs and interests of all the children, able and less able.'

CASE STUDY 3: TALK IN THE NURSERY

In 1991 a group of teachers of nursery children decided to include in their work a more intensive focus specifically on talk. They worked with small groups, arranging cover for each other to make it possible. They used picture-story books, rhyme and songs, listening games, toys and play-people, in such a way that children talked a great deal about detailed and specific aspects of the activity, and about themselves in relation to it. The teachers claimed that this work increased their own level of understanding of the children's development, concentration and frustration levels. It resulted in significant growth in children's self-esteem, their confidence in learning situations, and the length of time over which they could listen and concentrate.

(Adapted from Maggie Beech in *Special Children* No. 82, March 1995)

Increasing the frequency and status of talk in the classroom shifts the focus from what others can do for children towards how children can be enabled to speak, act and make decisions for themselves. There is a useful working distinction to be made between disability and handicap, where a handicap is seen to be the result of having a disability in an unadapted environment. Looking, therefore, at changes in the environment, as well as the needs of children, led teachers to an increased emphasis on strategies for encouraging purposeful talk.

Here is how teachers described their strategies and first steps:

(handwritten margin note: Nice because it)

- A public talk area which was comfortable and pleasant was provided. There, talk games could be played and talk opportunities created. It contained such things as a 'telling chair' which anyone could use when they had something to tell or retell, and a flip-chart onto which ideas could be brainstormed, or which a pupil could use to illustrate something in a report. Occasionally, we partnered pupils as they did these things, so that they could take encouragement from each other.

- We established a private talk area where pupils could discuss ideas, create stories, make tape recordings, or plan future work.

- We found ways of displaying talk, for example by taking photographs of the pupils at work, asking them to comment on what they were doing, and making a display of how they used talk to learn.

- In discussion and in planning with pupils, we focused upon the ways we use talk to learn.

- We reviewed pupils' own use of talk, working on using dialogue to tune in to their line of reasoning, giving them just enough structure to enable them to draw conclusions and make decisions.

- We made a conscious attempt to demonstrate in our listening and response that we valued what children had to say.

- We started with something other than language; for example, many children with poor word-finding competence have good visual abilities. Topics were presented in a way which exploited the visual as well as the linguistic channel.

Talk gives children the chance to establish and communicate a positive sense of identity. Views of self have a tendency to stick. They are applied not only to present learning, but also to expectations about future learning. Yet other children can be a powerful way of encouraging children to believe that they can be successful and to take pride in their achievements. They can, of course, be a powerful discouragement too, pressuring gifted children to hide their giftedness in order to avoid being seen as different. In an environment where they know that they are accepted and will be supported, where they have friends and shared loyalties, children are more likely to tackle learning with self-confidence and enthusiasm.

Here are some of the ways teachers involved pupils in supporting each other's learning:

- We negotiated rules for talk and listening with the children. Children discussed how they use talk in their learning and how they could help each other. Sometimes they drew up their own rules for talk, and used them to monitor their own and each other's behaviour.

- We took opportunities to confront children with the need to take responsibility for each other.

- We planned time for regular reports and discussions on how pupils were using talk.

- We gave outcomes of learning expressed through talk as much validity as those expressed through writing. Often, teachers were surprised by what pupils understood when they gave them increased opportunities to make an oral report. This also seemed to increase pupils' motivation to persevere with reading and writing. The oral report was an activity grasped frequently by very able children, as if they saw it as a chance to relate directly, in a friendly or informal way, to the rest of the class.

- We established a context in which pupils felt more confident to use talk. Teachers gave pupils time alone, to sit and think, or even 'think-write', before putting them with others. They worked from pairs to small friendship groups to larger, more impersonal situations, using the same material. A pupil would tell a story to a friend, retell it to a group of four, and finally present it to a group of mixed ages including adults.

MOVING ON

Varying the audience

If pupils are to talk to each other more frequently, how is it to be arranged? Teachers began to explore ways of managing groups in order that all children had the best possible access to learning. Sometimes children enter a phase where they see a particular area of learning as daunting. It may be reading, or number, or spelling, or handwriting, or speaking to a large group of children or adults. This experience can harden into a perception of themselves as failing, and what should have been a temporary difficulty can be extended, even generalized, across time and content. We all need to have achievement recognized, in order for it to affect the confidence with which we approach other tasks.

CASE STUDY 4: CHILDREN NOT TALKING

A teacher of Year 3 children was concerned that a number of the children were becoming increasingly isolated. They 'found it difficult to collaborate with others, or volunteer information.' She decided to organize a range of tasks and groupings, and to watch and listen carefully, and quickly noted that children responded more or less positively according to the make-up of the group. They were much more involved when in paired situations – whether with a friend or not – and would offer little in larger groupings. The teacher then asked the children to work in groups to carry out an experiment that would test how waterproof a brick was. The confident ones led the way, while the quieter ones either offered support or remained silent and apparently inactive. She then organized each child to report their activity individually to another child who was unfamiliar with the task. 'It was clear that the reticent ones gained a lot from the activity. They were able to sequence events very clearly, and indeed, some were able to hypothesize on what would happen if various materials were placed between the bricks.' One boy was aware that mud would not act as a waterproofing agent. He hadn't mentioned it in his group because the 'leader' was confident that mud was appropriate, but he offered the view quite freely when talking to one other child. 'It became obvious to me that the smaller the group initially, the more positive the response is likely to be. Children not talking does not mean children not listening, and learning, but when they talk I get to know more about what they really understand. And it's not just the strugglers; some of the brighter ones have surprised me with what they know.'

Many children identified as having special educational needs are separated from other children, either within or outside mainstream classrooms. Such separation can deny them full access to the National Curriculum and the support of other children, and emphasize their own sense of personal failure.

The 1992 HMI review showed teachers the extent to which withdrawing pupils into small groups restricted their curriculum and made for discontinuities in their learning. Too often, less able pupils of all ages are given a narrower range of experiences and opportunities in the National Curriculum for English than other pupils.

When children speak and listen to each other, aspects of their personal, emotional, and intellectual lives are brought into play simultaneously. Children with emotional and social difficulties, whatever their intellectual abilities, may initially find it hard to respond to a group-based task in ways which will demonstrate their true understanding and competence. Yet careful planning for talk can enable children to draw, often anecdotally, on their emotional and personal experience to help them to make sense of intellectual concepts.

Teachers set about creating a wider range of audiences for talk, whilst keeping the learning activity focused and purposeful.

- We arranged for pupils to use talk to *plan* their work before they set about it, to *share ideas* as they worked, and to *review and reflect upon* what they thought they had learned from the activity. This use of talk to plan, to do and to review was helpful to all pupils, but particularly valuable to those who needed support in approaching understanding.

- We planned learning activities which would require pupils to use others within the school as audiences or sources of information. This involved careful management and consultation, but provided diversity, interest and motivation for the pupils.

- We gave pupils opportunities to talk with one or two trusted friends about issues related to learning, such as things they found enjoyable, and things they found difficult in school.

- We built up the level of demand slowly, giving pupils a chance to work with one other person, or with pupils of the same sex, before placing them within larger or gender-mixed groups.

- We found ways of varying the talk-role of the children, for example, by asking them to work with older or younger pupils.

- We made sure that children were quite clear of the purposes for talk. We discussed with them why they were being asked to do things, how long they'd got, and what outcomes were expected. We enabled groups to send envoys to other children or groups, or to the teacher, if they needed clarification or more information.

- We explored the potential of the tape recorder in encouraging children to use talk effectively. For example, using the tape recorder as a 'note book', picking up pupils' conversation so that they can listen to it later and select the information they want to use; swapping information between classes or groups of children in different parts of the school or country; making verbal reports of a science experiment; verbally drafting ideas for writing.

- In science, history, geography – wherever there was challenging and potentially complex language associated with the knowledge – we used paired, co-operative reading to help children to share their understanding of text by explaining it and commenting upon it as they read.

Teachers of children with language-related difficulties customarily point to weaknesses such as a limited ability to structure language into coherent sequences, and to use language over an extended period with confidence and fluency. In an attempt to address this issue, and to build a bridge between oracy and literacy, teachers often embarked on promoting story-telling within their classes.

CASE STUDY 5: A STORY

William, who had great difficulty in writing, soon emerged as an eager and able story-teller, and asked if he could make up a story on his own. He was given a tape recorder and blank cassette, and he set about his task. William would go off to record privately, taking time to consider his ideas before committing them to tape. Hearing, and eventually reading, his own words was something of a shock to William. 'Did I really say all that?' Now he had a means of making language where he could achieve real success in his own eyes and in the eyes of others, and where he could show his considerable creative competence and awareness of structure and style.

IN FULL SWING

Thinking about tasks

Through talk, children can influence the pace and focus of their learning. They are able to go over things again in different ways and check out their perceptions against what others think. Talk allows them to concentrate attention on those areas where they need most help.

What is critical to this is setting learning tasks which make purposeful talk essential. As well as enabling teachers to diagnose what children find difficult in the context of what they have achieved, it is often the primary, sometimes the only, means through which many children can best communicate what they know and understand.

While some children may continue to require statements modifying specific aspects of the National Curriculum, there is no reason why, given the necessary resources and support, children of widely mixed abilities should not be taught together for much of the school day. HMI in 1992 reported that where children were accustomed to having their contributions listened to seriously and had gained confidence, work in groups of mixed ability helped to spread such confidence to others.

CASE STUDY 6: FRIENDS

A class of Year 5 children was asked to work with a class of Year 2 children on a science programme, exploring insects. They were organized into fours, two from each class. The teachers called them 'big friends and little friends'. As a group, they were allowed to look at books together, to explore a patch of garden outside the school, and to make a book of their discoveries. The teachers' comments demonstrate the extent to which able and less-able children in both year groups profited from the experience.

'I was surprised at the change in the way the older ones talked. They summarized, questioned, encouraged, and gave space and praise in ways I'd never seen them do before. I noticed a greater confidence and motivation in those pupils who normally struggled, or were reluctant learners.'

'My Year 2s were thrilled to have big friends. It gave them an audience which they valued, and led to longer stories, descriptions and explanations from them. Even the quiet children seemed more ready to talk to their older partner, and the more able children responded with genuine enthusiasm.'

'I noticed how some of my less able Year 5s spent much longer on the learning tasks when working with the other three. The fact that they were older seemed to give them status, and they were anxious to get a grasp of things in order to explain them.'

'Sometimes they worked in pairs instead of fours, perhaps looking at a book together. The older children were able to look at picture books, and use the same contextual clues for their reading as the younger ones. In every case, it helped them to realize how much they could do, and how much progress they had made since they were in Year 2.'

'The Year 2s were not overawed by the older ones. They talked a lot, told personal stories, asked questions and made suggestions. Sometimes they lost interest, but not often, and, I think, less often than they do in normal classroom circumstances.'

Throughout the programme, the teachers listened, took notes and photographs, and used these to make a report to the children at the end. This was done back in their own classes. The children were also given time to talk about what they had learned (in the Year 2 class as a whole class; in the Year 5 class in small groups, which then brainstormed their comments as a class).

There is strong evidence that group work, when organized well and focused rigorously on task, in no way disadvantages able children, yet significantly helps the less able.

What was happening in those schools where talk and learning had been carefully integrated? First, it had taken time to achieve the levels of confidence and involvement that were apparent. It had needed incremental steps from small beginnings in classrooms towards an agreed policy at whole-school level.

Second, schools had made an effort to create a consensus view about the value of talk which could be reflected in the life of the school beyond the classroom through assemblies, uses of space, class and school councils, an increased and focused involvement of parents and those who work in the school.

Third, talk was being planned into the learning. Thought was given to ways of using paired activities, the composition and membership of groups, and the purposes for collaborative work. There was clear and regular provision for four areas of talk experience which are particularly important in enabling children to take advantage of talk to help them in their learning:

1. Exploratory talk, where children use their own and each other's ideas to approach understanding.

2. Talk to reinforce learning, where pupils are required to retell or re-explain what they have learned or found out. In doing so, they reappraise their own understanding, and refine the language in which it is expressed.

3. Talk to present to a larger audience, where pupils undertake a more extended, formal statement of what they have learned or wish to communicate.

4. Talk to reflect, where pupils review what they have done, what they have achieved, and what they need to work on more.

Fourth, teachers arranged for the able and less able to work together on occasions, in ways which enabled all children to have a role and make a positive contribution. For example, teachers organized for pupils to work together in order to present their findings to other pupils who needed the information to complete their own work. In a jigsaw activity, more gifted or less able pupils worked with others in an expert group, finding out about a specific aspect of a topic. Then each individual member of that group would be required to go back to their original home group as the only person with this particular piece of knowledge.

Finally, teachers were particularly concerned to use talk for reflection. Children would be asked to prepare together a summary and comment on what they had achieved or discovered. It provided opportunities to review what had been learned and how it was achieved; it enabled pupils to have their progress recognized and supported by others, and to set realistic goals for the future without a sense of embarrassment or personal inferiority.

To be effective in supporting the learning of both the gifted and the less able pupil, the experience of talk must be both central and wide-ranging. Here are the ideas which two teachers in one special school generated as they reviewed the provision for talk in their school.

WE NEED TO THINK ABOUT:

- Children talking to familiar adults.
- Involving adults outside the classroom to give children different audiences.
- Children talking to children – peers and others.
- Reports to peers and others.
- Time for groups to reflect upon what they have done.
- Talking in pairs:
  – incidental talk;
  – organizational talk;
  – role play (imaginative talk);
  – instructional talk.
- Questioning – encouraging children to ask questions of the teacher and of each other.
- Observing children's talk outside the classroom, e.g. playground, swimming, dinner-time.
- Talking at home, with their parents recording.
- Using jigsawing to give children special areas of knowledge to share with others.
- Drawing up agreed guidelines for teacher self-appraisal.
- Identifying individual children in turn to watch and listen to them as they work.
- Tape recording and playing back with the child(ren).
- Video-taping, as a means of children presenting what they have learned, and of reviewing their work.
- Using photography, from which children mount a display, explaining what they were doing and how talk helped.

The ways of working, and the quality of response from pupils, described in this chapter will only begin to happen over time. Teachers must begin gradually, choosing a particular area to try, and extending the range of strategies as confidence grows. There will also be times when it doesn't seem to be working – children have to learn how to operate collaboratively, and, like adults, some will find it hard. They need time and a growing familiarity with these ways of working to take full advantage of the uses of talk in learning. But a well-planned focus on talk yields significant results, both in the development of competence in literacy and in children's sense of their own status as learners.

KEY POINTS

Status for talk encourages those for whom reading and writing are difficult.

Ensure equal opportunities and access to the curriculum through oracy.

Negotiate rules for speaking and listening so that everyone can contribute.

Teachers' Notes 1

GUIDELINES FOR INSET LEADER

A whole-school staff development programme for speaking and listening and children with special needs

1. In pairs, discuss and agree on two ways in which your school/department could involve pupils with special educational needs more fully in learning, through talk. In fours, share your two points with another pair, justifying your decisions. The groups of four present their comments to the rest. One person lists publicly the main suggestions.

2. The whole staff choose two of the issues from the list as the ones on which to focus.

3. Planning groups of two or three develop one activity/strategy (school or classroom) to try as a way of responding to each of the two issues identified. The groups report their plans and agree to try them.

A *short* trial period is given – as short as is considered reasonable, but it should be no more than two weeks, or the impetus is lost.

4. Reporting back. Staff share their experiences in their original planning group, and then present their experience and recommendations to the whole staff.

5. Staff discussion. From this experience, what should we implement as a permanent feature of the school's work?

This cycle can be repeated from Stage 4 if the list initially generated is sufficiently rich in issues and suggestions.

Photocopiable Sheet 1

A WHOLE-SCHOOL STAFF DEVELOPMENT PROGRAMME

1. Two ways in which your school/department could involve pupils with special educational needs more fully in learning, through talk:

    a)

    b)

2. Two issues chosen by the whole staff upon which we could focus:

    a)

    b)

3. Strategies or activities to try in response to the above issues:

After a trial period:

4. Reporting back:

Teachers' Notes 2

GUIDELINES FOR INSET LEADER

Staff development: reflecting on learning through talk

Consideration of a video of talk and learning from the point of view of the pupils as learners, and of the teacher as manager of the learning and monitor of speaking and listening.

You will need an appropriate piece of video. It can be made by one of the teachers, working with one or more children, or it can be chosen from a range of commercial material available.

Groups of three are formed. Each group is allocated either Task 1 or Task 2.

Task 1. How are the children using talk to learn? Track the changes of audience, or task or focus through the video. Try to see what happens through the eyes of the pupils. How is their use of language helping them to approach and clarify understanding? What is their talk telling you about how they learn and how they use language?

Task 2. What is the role of the teacher? Track the things she does and says through the video. How is she trying to manage/enable the use of talk to learn? How does she try to monitor and assess speaking and listening? What planning and organization has gone into the activity?

• Groups watch the video, and take notes in relation to the allocated task.
• After viewing, groups discuss observations.
• Groups who have had the same task come together and brainstorm a list in response to the questions:

Task 1 – HOW ARE THE CHILDREN LEARNING?

Task 2 – HOW IS THE TEACHER HELPING AND MONITORING THE CHILDREN'S WORK?

Plenary – a person representing each of the two tasks shares observations with the rest of the whole-group and accepts responses from others.

STAFF DEVELOPMENT:
REFLECTING ON LEARNING THROUGH TALK

Task 1: focus on children	Task 2: focus on teacher
How are the children learning?	How is the teacher helping and monitoring the children' work?
Track the changes of audience, or task or focus through the video.	Track the things the teacher does and says through the video.
Try to see what happens through the eyes of the pupils.	How is she trying to manage/ enable the use of talk to learn?
How is their use of language helping them to approach and clarify understanding?	How does the teacher try to monitor and assess speaking and listening?
What is their talk telling you about how they learn and how they use language?	What planning and organization have gone into the activity?

This sheet can form the basis for staff discussion, a video of a lesson having been shown to the staff.

Chapter 12

Tracking Talk

Diana Cinamon and Sally Elding

The authors are experienced teachers who have worked in the 'early years' as well as the older primary age range. They both worked as Co-ordinators with the National Oracy Project (1988–1991) through which they supported teachers in developing good practice in speaking and listening approaches in the classroom, looking particularly at the recording and assessment process.

BACKGROUND

The process of assessment advocated here is to build a profile of a child's talk in the same way as a folder of writing might be collated over a period of time to demonstrate achievement. The profile will contain descriptions of talk in various contexts, comment, action plans and a summary of achievement. It may also contain information gained from interviews with parents and pupils' own talk records or diaries.

The word 'talk' is used in this chapter to refer to the interactive processes of speaking and listening. The special nature of talk presents a challenge for those assessing spoken language. Some of the reasons for this are due to the nature of talk itself. It is over in a moment, it changes according to the purpose for which it is used or who is speaking, or where. This means that the process of assessment has to be appropriate for talk and be adaptable to a wide range of circumstances.

How to measure progress is equally challenging. Children's talk obviously progresses in the primary years, but until recently there has been a lack of interest in the speech of primary school children, especially when compared with research done on the language of under-fives. This is partly due to the focus on written rather than spoken language but perhaps also due to the fact that there are no clear markers of development to measure the precise extent of the growth with resulting scores and quotients. The National Oracy Project and the advent of the Speaking and Listening component in the National Curriculum has helped focus attention on what can usefully be gained by monitoring and assessing talk.

How children talk has always influenced teachers' opinions of children's achievements. One of the difficulties when assessing talk is to separate pupils' knowledge and understanding of a subject and their ability to talk about it. The distinction between the assessment *of* talk and assessing *through* talk is a useful one. Information gained through tracking children's talk can be used for the assessment of different areas of the curriculum, and sometimes what a child has to say will be the only way to check understanding.

While tracking talk is not easy, the process involved has positive outcomes. Increased knowledge about speaking and listening and efforts to make explicit the criteria on which assessment is based enables teachers to have a more objective basis for making judgements. It also helps them to cater for individual needs, inform short- and long-term planning as well as provide evidence for record-keeping.

The ability to communicate goes beyond talking and listening, and for some pupils touch, gesture, facial expression or the ability to 'sign' may be the paramount means of using language. Many of the ideas and suggestions in this chapter are sufficiently flexible to be used with children who have special needs. They are also applicable for the particular experience and needs of bilingual children, including those new to English.

AIMS

The purpose of this chapter is to provide teachers with a practical and manageable guide to the assessment of speaking and listening. It should be appropriate for the assessment of children throughout the primary school and be equally valid for pupils with different needs and experiences.

STARTING OUT

The curriculum

Other chapters in this book are concerned with how to promote and develop speaking and listening in the classroom; those ideas will provide opportunities for the assessment of talk. In all areas of the curriculum children are required to use talk as a tool for learning. They need to know that talk is valued and experience a curriculum organized so that talk is used for a variety of purposes. In order to develop their skills with a range of audiences they need experience of working in varied groups and of talking to different people. To gain a full picture of children's abilities it is essential to have examples of their talk in different situations.

Curriculum planning should therefore include broad objectives to ensure that the teaching of subject areas will enable pupils to talk for a variety of purposes. The demands of tasks, and how these are organized, shape talking and listening opportunities and responses.

Detailed planning of activities and tasks should be specific as to the audiences involved, which means considering who the children will be talking to and for what purpose. The organization of groups is one aspect. For instance, a large group requires considerable skill in negotiating roles and organizing tasks whereas a pair can take turns and discuss with more ease. Cultural or language backgrounds need also to be taken into account. There may be times when a bilingual group will enable pupils to use a shared home language providing mutual support, while at other times a mixed language group may provide a necessary stimulus. The gender of a group may also affect the outcome. Girls will often participate more freely in a technology or science task without the presence of boys. Groups selected for ability can provide for specific needs. For example, reluctant or hesitant speakers may feel able to participate when their more confident peers are absent, whereas dominant pupils put together may benefit from learning to cope with the contributions of those with similar traits.

In order to have a true picture, pupils' speaking and listening should be observed over a period of time and in different contexts. The learning experiences within the school and the models for talking and listening provided by teachers will significantly affect achievement. *What* children talk about reflects the interests, activities and concerns of the age group involved and the tasks they are given to do. *How* they talk depends significantly on the opportunities they have been given to gain experience in different talk contexts.

How well children listen should only be judged from observing them in a variety of contexts and at best can only be inferred from their responses and behaviour. Children who may appear not to listen are often responding to situations which are of little interest to them, or it may be their behaviour which is the problem rather than an inability to listen and understand. The assessment of their listening skills must not be confined to their willingness to listen to teachers talking, often at some length, to large groups. When a pupil's listening is a cause for concern she or he should be observed in situations which require them to talk, listen and respond to others, particularly their peers. Young children who have consistent difficulty or poor articulation should be checked for hearing loss.

Attitudes to language

Assessments of children's language need to be as objective as possible if judgements made are to be fair. In a society which is particularly sensitive to social class, responses to talk are conditioned as much by attitudes to accent and dialect as they are by the effectiveness of the communication. Those assessing spoken language need to be aware of any prejudices they may have. The first concern should be with the meanings children express and the repertoire they have for learning and communicating.

As the use of Standard English is now required in the primary school, the distinction between accent and dialect must be understood by teachers and children. Children's sense of identity comes from their family and community, and how they speak is part of that. To *add* to pupils' modes of speech should be the aim so that they can eventually function in different parts of society. Children have considerable knowledge about language gained from the community and the media, and need to know about the place of Standard English in our society and in what way it is similar to or different from their own spoken forms.

The value for bilingual children of continuing to use their home language in the classroom as they learn English is well established. Unfortunately, the National Curriculum requires only the assessment of English rather than language development in general, failing to recognize and give credit to the linguistic achievements of bilingual children. However, their profiles should contain information about the languages they speak or understand.

MOVING ON

Evidence for assessment

Assessment must be based on evidence to be valid and provide information which teachers can use for the benefit of their pupils. This evidence will need to be collected from 'real situations'. Due to 'talk' requiring someone to talk to and something to talk about, the type of assessment which is set up in the corridor is not likely to be fruitful. Planning for assessment needs therefore to be part of planning the curriculum and is most effective if incorporated in a whole school approach. There is an example of a whole-school workshop on assessment in this chapter.

Children should be aware that their speaking and listening are assessed and be involved in the process where possible. They need to know what is expected of them and to have appropriate use of language valued and praised so they have models to work from. Children will behave and speak differently when with their peers, so recordings made when adults are *not* present are particularly revealing. Children can be involved in assessing their own progress; a work-card for this purpose is provided on page 218.

Collecting evidence is best separated from the process of *evaluating the achievement* which should be done subsequently. Trying to decide the level of fluency, for example, or the relevance of a pupil's talk while trying to keep track of what is being said, is too confusing. Notes or recordings of pupils' speech need to be taken. It is generally better to describe what a child says or write down samples of their talk rather than to try and fit their speech into a checklist. Usually an observation will be planned in advance, but occasionally notes will be made because something noteworthy has occurred. Comments such as 'She used a good tone of voice', or 'He interrupted too often', which indicate *how* the talk proceeded as well as samples of speech, can also be included in the notes which will help with the analysis. If bilingual children are 'code switching' and the observer does not understand the language, notes can indicate what the purpose of their talk is likely to be, or what caused them to move into another language, etc. Bilingual staff may undertake this aspect.

Do not be surprised if different talk behaviour is observed from that expected. Language is flexible and different ways of talking can be triggered by events.

Collecting evidence

What are the tasks?
The children may be carrying out a variety of tasks such as:

* Painting a picture with a friend.
* Telling a story to a group.
* Reporting to a group on an experiment undertaken.
* Playing in the home corner.
* Explaining to the teacher how maths was done.
* Speculating on why a model collapsed.
* Estimating height and weight within a group.
* Giving instructions to a partner.
* Describing an unusual object as accurately as possible.
* Talking in a class assembly.

CASE STUDY 1: A PIGEON

Familiarity with subject matter affects confidence and fluency.

Debbie, not renowned for her speech, brought a pigeon into school: she *displayed knowledge* of the bird's behaviour; *described* how to care for it; *explained* about the process of homing; *introduced* the class to new *terminology* and *showed* a remarkable *sense* of how to talk to her *audience*.

Who are the children talking to?
A range of audiences such as:

- partner, teacher, known adult or unknown adult;
- older child, self or younger child;
- ability group, random group, gender group or home language group;
- friendship group, class or school.

How is the evidence to be collected?
- Verbatim notes of children's speech.
- 'Post it' pads and small note-books are handy.
- Speaking and Listening sheet.
- Tape recordings. (Only tape-record if conditions are right. If you have not tried tape recording before you will find children need time to get used to it. A cloth under the recorder helps cut background noise.)

When is the evidence to be collected?
This must be *over a period of time* in order to build a profile of the child's spoken language abilities and to measure progress and development.

Where shall it be done?
- Playground.
- Classroom.
- P.E.
- Library.
- Visits.
- School office, etc.

Who will collect the evidence?

- Teachers.
- Classroom assistants.
- Bilingual assistants.
- Nursery nurses.
- Other adults.
- Parents.
- Children.

Parents can discuss their children's talk, perhaps in the form of an interview such as that described in The Primary Language Record (ILEA: 1988).

Evidence from children can be acquired by discussing their 'talk' with them or from classroom work such as a Talk Diary or work-card such as the one below.

WORK-CARD

Children's assessment of themselves and their peers

When you have finished your talk activity work with a partner to consider the following:

How well did you listen to each other?

Was there an opportunity for everyone to say something?

Were there times when you did not keep to the point?

How did talk help you to complete the task?

Did you achieve what you set out to do?

Did anyone dominate the talk? Was this helpful?

What was really interesting or important?

Were there disagreements? How were these resolved?

Did you reject any ideas? If so, why?

What would you do differently next time?

IN FULL SWING

A whole-school approach

As with all forms of assessment, a whole-school approach is the best way to ensure that methods used result from a consensus of opinion. This is particularly important for the assessment of talk, as there is such divergence and strength of opinion about spoken language. Assessing talk is also a new field for many. Staff need the opportunity to find points of agreement and work out differences. One way to develop a whole-school approach is to include assessment workshops as part of the school development plan. Bilingual and other support staff should be included. The purpose of those workshops could be:

- To share views, attitudes and ideas about talk and its role in children's learning.
- To work towards a consensus about assessment, and how to incorporate this into curriculum planning.
- To decide how to collect and store information.
- To make plans for future development.

Teachers' workshop

Directions for leader or organizer

Warm-up activity
1. Organize the staff into small groups and ask them to discuss their own talk experiences, starting with their earliest memories. Appoint one member of each group to observe and to write down anything she or he notices about the communication between group members. Observers feed back to the whole group to stimulate discussion.
2. Discuss accent and dialect, the position of Standard English and other varieties of English.

Sharing children's talk
For this session you need to have gathered some examples of children's talk to share with colleagues. (Photocopy and use the Speaking and Listening record sheet for this: ***Photocopiable Sheet 3***.)

1. Work in pairs on extracts you find interesting. Consider the following:
   a) What are the children able to do?

b) Is the talk what you would expect from the task set? If not, why not?

c) What would you want to identify for assessment purposes?
(Try using the Key Skills section of the Talk Repertoire sheet: ***Photo-copiable Sheet 1.***)

2.   Regroup as a whole staff to share what you have learned.

3.   Identify areas for further staff development.

PROGRESS AND DEVELOPMENT

Reviewing the evidence

Talk is such a commonplace accomplishment and used for so many purposes that deciding what to look for when assessing can seem daunting. Studies of children's talk and what they do at various stages abound up to the age of five, but the picture subsequently becomes much less clear. By the age of five, children have most of the grammar of the language in place. What then is the progress they make as they grow older and how can speaking and listening be assessed?

A working definition of 'progress' can be the pupil gaining increasing control over his or her language to a wider range of audiences, for a greater variety of purposes and in different settings.

More specific indicators are needed to see how that control is developed. To provide a starting-point, the Key Skills section of the Talk Repertoire sheet has been devised using the Programmes of Study and Attainment Targets for Speaking and Listening Key Stages 1 and 2 as guidance for what is expected of children at these stages. This section can be used as the basis for evaluating progress and development. However, any list concerned with talk is bound to be limited so other achievements will inevitably be observed and these should be added to the pupil's record.

The evidence gathered provides feedback about the progress of individual children, but more importantly it reveals a great deal about how children learn.

Benefits of assessing speaking and listening

The benefits of a more explicit approach to the assessment of speaking and listening for both teacher and pupil are that it:

•   reveals achievement in all subject areas;

•   makes clear what children can do so that their experience can be extended;

•   increases understanding of how talk operates in different contexts;

- develops awareness of teachers' own talk and how they interact with pupils;

- involves children in monitoring their own talk and that of their peers;

- increases understanding of how bilingual children use their languages;

- informs teachers about children's concept development, knowledge and understanding.

What is found through the process of assessment can be used to:

- recognize achievement and diagnose difficulties;

- provide evidence for records;

- inform planning;

- inform parents;

- provide feedback to the child;

- satisfy the requirements of the National Curriculum.

KEY POINTS

A whole-school approach to assessment.

Structure your curriculum planning to include assessment of talk and listening.

Set out to learn about talk through listening to children and through discussion with colleagues.

Engage children in your assessment process and make them aware of the criteria being used.

Support children's talking and listening by organizing opportunities to use talk for learning.

Start planning to collect children's talk evidence over a period of time.

Make time to observe a variety of groupings, different tasks and audiences.

Evidence needs reviewing and summarizing.

Note down examples of children's talk using note-pads, tape recorders, etc.

Think how you can feed back your findings into future plans.

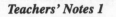

Teachers' Notes 1

HOW TO USE THE ASSESSMENT SHEETS

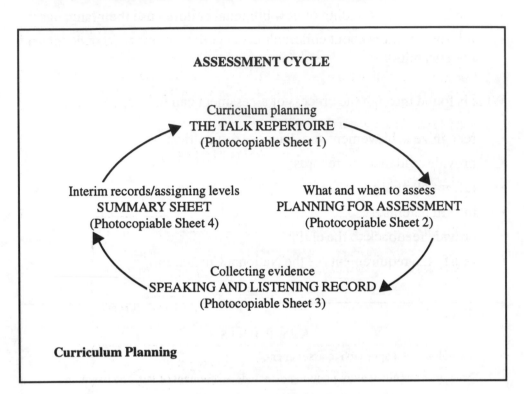

Use Photocopiable Sheet 1 when you are planning your work. Highlight the speaking and listening *purposes* and *audiences* you intend to focus on.

Repeat this process each term using a different colour or code to show coverage over a year. Used as an aide-memoire in this way the Talk Repertoire will help you incorporate talking and listening into your overall and detailed curriculum planning.

CASE STUDY 2: TERM-BY-TERM PLANNING

The learning for the autumn term for a Year 4 class was based around a scientific topic/theme. The purposes and audiences are *underlined* in this illustration. The *circled* examples show the planning for the spring term when the pupils prepared and told stories to a younger age group.

The Talk Repertoire

Class **4**
Year **1995/6** Autumn, (Spring) Summer

Range of Purposes

(tell)	explore	develop	(ask)	(answer)	argue
clarify	discuss	plan	recall	justify	report
predict	(describe)	respond	investigate		persuade
observe	comment	(present)		speculate	
explain	reason	extend	(reflect)	converse	evaluate

Audiences

(friend) teacher known adult
unknown adult older child (self) (younger child)
ability group (random group) gender group
bilingual group (friendship group) (class) school

Key Skills

fluency coherence clarity confidence articulation
relevance appropriateness thoughtfulness precision

express ideas convey opinions extend ideas add detail
contribute to discussion take turns adapt to audience

describe accurately tell a story hold a conversation
recall an event reflect on experience organise thoughts
clarify evaluate question respond

uses appropriate vocabulary tone pace style grammar

Photocopiable Sheet 1

THE TALK REPERTOIRE

Class: _____

Year: _____   **Autumn**   **Spring**   **Summer**

Range of purposes

tell	explore	develop	ask	answer	argue
clarify	discuss	plan	recall	justify	report
predict	describe	respond	investigate		persuade
observe	comment		present	speculate	
explain	reason	extend	reflect	converse	evaluate

Audiences

friend   teacher   known adult

unknown adult   older child   self   younger child

ability group   random group   gender group

bilingual group   friendship group   class   school

Key Skills

fluency   coherence   clarity   confidence   articulation

relevance   appropriateness   thoughtfulness   precision

express ideas   convey opinions   extend ideas   add detail

contribute to discussion   take turns   adapt to audience

describe accurately   tell a story   hold a conversation

recall an event   reflect on experience   organize thoughts

clarify   evaluate   question   respond

uses appropriate vocabulary   tone   pace   style   grammar

Teachers' Notes 2

WHAT AND WHEN TO ASSESS

Select activities or tasks which will give children the chance to use talk for a range of purposes and plot this on the 'Planning for Assessment' sheet (Photocopiable Sheet 2).

Note down what the assessment opportunities are likely to be. You can either get information about the group or focus on one child's skills.

This list can be used to check the tasks and breadth of evidence to be collected.

Children will be engaged in activities which involve:

- getting along with peers, getting things done, sharing resources and materials;
- making contributions, taking turns, listening to others, planning and organizing as a member of a group;
- telling stories or anecdotes;
- asking and answering questions, giving and receiving instructions;
- conversing with peers, with teachers and other adults;
- making observations, commenting, describing objects, people, events;
- sorting out ideas, solving problems, developing understanding, speculating about events or processes;
- putting forward a point of view, arguing a case, justifying opinions;
- expressing feelings, emotions or appreciation;
- presenting work to a group, class or the whole school;
- reflecting on events, experiences or on work done;
- adapting talk to suit the needs of the listener, such as a foreign visitor or younger child.

CASE STUDY 3: RED RIDING HOOD

As one of a range of activities covering all curriculum areas based around the story of Red Riding Hood, pupils in a Year 1 class made a model of Grandma's house and then had to explain to another group what they had done. When making the model they would be expected to plan, discuss and explore ideas and solve problems within the group. A different set of talking and listening skills would be used when telling others about their work.

Planning for Assessment

Activities	Audience(s)	Range of Purposes	Assessment Opportunities
Red Riding Hood Red Group Make a model of grandma's house.	Each other (Ability group)	Plan, negotiate, organise, discuss, explore,	Make notes on the groups initial planning talk - 5-10 minutes. Photocopy for each child's file.
Explain how model was made.	Random group	Explain, present, describe, answer	Allow time for presentation. Note the listening skills of the audience.

This example shows the plans the Year 1 teacher made for this unit of work, using Photocopiable Sheet 2, 'Planning for Assessment'.

PLANNING FOR ASSESSMENT

Term: _____   Year: _____

Activities	Audience(s)	Range of purposes	Assessment opportunities

---

Teachers' Notes 3

COLLECTING EVIDENCE

Collect evidence for the Speaking and Listening Record (Photocopiable Sheet 3).

You can plan in advance to take notes of an activity, or alternatively do this when you notice something interesting happening.

This sheet provides the evidence which enables you to compile a profile of a child's speech. At some stage you will need to decide how much evidence you need in order to make an informed assessment. Children whose progress is a cause for concern may need more assessments for their problems to be diagnosed and appropriate action taken.

The notes made could be samples of speech, with a description of how the talk progressed. Either write directly onto the sheet as you observe or transfer information from rough notes. In the example below, a tape recording of pupils' talk provides the evidence.

The comment column should be completed using the written evidence and the KEY SKILLS section of the Talk Repertoire Sheet for guidance as to the skills demonstrated and action needed.

In those instances when the observer is *not* the teacher, the comment column may need to be completed as a result of a discussion between the observer and teacher. Decide in advance how this is to be done.

In the following example, pupils made a tape recording as one part of the task set. A transcript of the first part of the recording is printed. The information gathered here was used for the Speaking and Listening Record of all three girls involved, the transcript clipped onto the back of the sheet to save copying the speech onto the record.

CASE STUDY 4: MOVEMENT

As part of a science and technology topic on 'Movement', three Year 5 girls were given specifications and resources for making a four-wheeled buggy. Once they were satisfied they could make it, they were to try to:

    a) make the buggy roll down a slope in a straight line;
    b) make the buggy safe on impact with a plastic brick wall;
    c) make the passenger (a pen top) stay safely in the seat on impact with the wall.

Then they taped a discussion of how they made and tested the buggy, for a reporting session to the class later in the day.

Transcript

F: Well first of all we got a piece of card and cut it up into two 5cm circles and two . . . I think it was 3cm circles.

A: Yes and then we had this piece of long card and we got two bulldog clips and we put them on the ends.

S: And then we got . . .

A: Yes and then we got the wheels . . .

S: Yes we got some tiny wooden things . . .

A: . . . and we got some small lollipop sticks . . . we got those small lollipop things and . . . we stuck the pieces of wood circles onto the lollipop things as the wheels with drawing pins.

F: Because first of all when we tried it the bulldog clips kept leaning to the left and right so we stuck plasticine in the middle and the outside so it wouldn't and that worked okay.

S: We tried three bumpers and the last one we tried, the one we've got now is a balloon and it worked.

*   And had . . . yes we had to do this task and we had to make a seat and we had to put a felt tipped pen in it . . .*

F: We used the lid of a felt tipped pen.

A: . . . yes and it had to be unsafe and . . .

F: Me and Anne had a massive argument about it.

Photocopiable Sheet 3

SPEAKING AND LISTENING RECORD

Name   Background details

Age

Class   Special needs

Activity	Observer	Date
Audience(s)		
Notes	Comments	

Activity	Observer	Date
Audience(s)		
Notes	Comments	

Teachers' Notes 4

SUMMARY SHEETS: ASSIGNING NC LEVELS

At the end of the year information should be transferred to the Summary Sheet (Photocopiable Sheet 4) from the Speaking and Listening Record together with any other evidence obtained.

The summary provides a record of what has been achieved and any action that still needs to be taken. Completing the summary sheet once or twice in a year should be sufficient for most purposes. Additional interim records may be necessary for a minority of children.

Use the Summary Sheet and the National Curriculum Attainment Targets for guidance when assigning a level.

Evaluate achievement to date and plan your programme for the child for the rest of the year. The record will enable you to report to parents and work with them to overcome difficulties.

SUMMARY SHEET

Teacher Class	Name Home language Date of birth Other relevant information
Interim record of achievements	Date Areas where progress needed
Summary	Date Areas where progress needed N.C. level

NATIONAL CURRICULUM ATTAINMENT TARGET 1: SPEAKING AND LISTENING (DfEE: 1995)

Level 1

Pupils talk about matters of immediate interest. They listen to others and usually respond appropriately. They convey simple meanings to a range of listeners, speaking audibly, and begin to extend their ideas or accounts by providing some detail.

Level 2

Pupils begin to show confidence in talking and listening, particularly where the topics interest them. On occasions, they show awarenesss of the needs of the listener by including relevant detail. In developing and explaining their ideas they speak clearly and use a growing vocabulary. They usually listen carefully and respond with increasing appropriateness to what others say. They are beginning to be aware that in some situations a more formal vocabulary and tone of voice are used.

Level 3

Pupils talk and listen confidently in different contexts, exploring and communicating ideas. In discussion, they show understanding of the main points. Through relevant comments and questions, they show they have listened carefully. They begin to adapt what they say to the needs of the listener, varying the use of vocabulary and the level of detail. They are beginning to be aware of Standard English and when it is used.

Level 4

Pupils talk and listen with confidence in an increasing range of contexts. Their talk is adapted to the purpose; developing ideas thoughtfully, describing events and conveying their opinions clearly. In discussion, they listen carefully, making contributions and asking questions that are responsive to others' ideas and views. They use appropriately some of the features of standard English vocabulary and grammar.

Level 5

Pupils talk and listen confidently in a wide range of contexts, including some that are of a formal nature. Their talk engages the interest of the listener as they begin to vary their expression and vocabulary. In discussion, they pay close attention to what others say, ask questions to develop ideas and make contributions that take account of others' views. They begin to use Standard English in formal situations.

Level 6

Pupils adapt their talk to the demands of different contexts with increasing confidence. Their talk engages the interest of the listener through the variety of its vocabulary and expression. Pupils take an active part in discussion, showing understanding of ideas and sensitivity to others. They are usually fluent in their use of Standard English in formal situations.

Bibliography and Further Reading

Andrews, R. (1995) *Teaching and Learning Argument*. Cassell.

Baddeley, G. (ed.) (1992) *Learning Together Through Talk*. Hodder and Stoughton.

Bain, R. (1992) *Looking Into Language*. Hodder and Stoughton.

Baker, C. (1995) *A Parents' and Teachers' Guide to Bilingualism*. Multilingual Matters.

Bruce, T. (1991) *Time to Play in Early Childhood Education*. Hodder and Stoughton.

Cam, P. (1995) *Thinking Together: Philosophical Inquiry in the Classroom*. Australian Teaching Association and Hale and Ironmonger.

Carrington, B. and Troyna, B. (1988) *Children and Controversial Issues*. Falmer Press.

Chambers, A. (1994) *Tell Me – Children, Reading and Talk*. Thimble Press.

Chesterfield, R. and K. (1985) 'Natural Order in Children's Use of Second Language Learning Strategies', in *Applied Linguistics*. Vol. 6 No. 1, Spring.

Corson, D. (1988) *Oral Language Across the Curriculum*. Multilingual Matters.

Corson, D. (1990) *Language Policy Across the Curriculum*. Multilingual Matters.

Cullingford, C. (1991) *The Inner World of the School: Children's Ideas About School*. Cassell.

DfEE (1995) *English in the National Curriculum*. HMSO.

Dunne, E. and Bennett, N. (1990) *Talking and Learning in Groups*. Macmillan.

Edwards, V. (1996) *Speaking and Listening in Multilingual Classrooms*. University of Reading.

First Steps Oral Language Continuum/Resource Book (1997). Heinemann.

Fisher, R. (1996) *Stories for Thinking*. Nash Pollock.

Galton, M. and Williamson, J. (1992) *Groupwork on the Primary Classroom*. Routledge.

Geekie, P. and Raban, B. (1993) *Learning to Read and Write Through Talk*. Trentham Books.

Graves, D. (1983) *Writing: Children and Teachers at Work*. Heinemann.

Hall, N. (1989) *Writing with Reason*. Hodder & Stoughton.

HMI (1990) *The Teaching and Learning of Drama*. HMSO.

HMI (1992) *Special Educational Needs Report*. HMSO.

Howe, A. (1997) *Making Talk Work*. NATE.

Howe, A. and Johnson, J. (1992) *Common Bonds: Storytelling in the Classroom*. Hodder and Stoughton.

ILEA (1988) *The Primary Language Record*. CLPE.

Jones, E. and Reynolds, G. (1992) *The Play's the Thing: Teachers' Roles in Children's Play*. Teachers' College Press.

Jones, P. (1988) *Lipservice. The Story of Talk in Schools*. Open University Press.

Kallie, J. (1991) *Structured Informality: ESOL 5–16*. Oxfordshire County Council.

Kitson, N. and Spiby, I. (1997) *Drama 7–11*. Routledge.

Lipman, M. (1991) *Thinking in Education*. Cambridge University Press (US).

Lipman, M. (1993) *Thinking, Children and Education*. Montclair, Kendall/Hunt.

Mayor, B. 'What Does it Mean to be Bilingual?' in Mercer, N. (1988) *Language and Literacy in the Primary School*. Open University.

Mills, R. W. and J. (1993) *Bilingualism in the Primary School*. Routledge.

Morgan, N. and Saxton, J. (1989) *Teaching Drama*. Stanley Thornes.

Moyles, J. (1994) *The Excellence of Play*. Open University Press.

Murris, K. (1992) *Teaching Philosophy with Picture Books*. Infonet Publications.

NCC (1992) *A Curriculum for All*. HMI Review. HMSO.

NCC Occasional Paper Number 6 (1992) *Oracy and Special Educational Needs*. HMSO.

NCC/NOP (1990) *Teaching, Talking and Learning in KS1/2*. HMSO.

NOP (1991) *Assessing Talk in KS1 and 2*. HMSO.

Neelands, J. (1992) *Learning Through Imagined Experience*. Hodder and Stoughton.

Norman, K. (1992) *Thinking Voices*. Hodder and Stoughton.

Nutbrown, C. (1994) *Threads of Thinking: Young Children Learning and the Role of Early Education*. Paul Chapman.

Open University (1991) *Talk and Learning 5–16*. Open University Press.

Powling, C. (1997) *Storytelling in Schools*. University of Reading.

Reah, D. (1998) *The Language of Newspapers*. Routledge.

Redfern, A. and Edwards, V. (1997) *Practical Ways to Inspire Young Authors*. University of Reading.

Robinson, O. and Thomas, G. (1988) *Tackling Learning Difficulties*. Hodder and Stoughton.

Ross, A. (1991) *Inspirations for Speaking and Listening*. Scholastic.

Slavin, R. (1990) *Cooperative Learning: Theory, Research and Practice*. Prentice Hall.

Tweddle, J. and Simpson, M. (1994) *A Language Map*. Section XI Support. Birmingham.

Vygotsky, L. (1978) *Mind in Society*. Harvard University Press.

Walsh, B. (1988) *Shut Up! Communication in the Secondary School*. Cassell.

Whitebread, D. (1996) *Language and Learning in the Early Years*. Routledge.

Whitehead, M. (1990) *Language and Literacy in the Early Years*. Paul Chapman.

Woolland, B. (1993) *The Teaching of Drama in the Primary School*. Longman.

Wragg, E. (1994) *An Introduction to Classroom Observation*. Routledge.

Index